RIDING THE HIGH WAVES OF LIFE

David S. Philemon

Royal Diadem Publishing Inc.

Dedication

To the Almighty God, my Rock, Refuge, and Source of all wisdom and strength. Thank You for Your unwavering love, grace, and the purpose You've placed within me. May this book bring glory to Your name and draw others closer to You.

And to my beloved spiritual parents, Dr. Paul and Dr. Mrs. Becky Paul Enenche, who have faithfully nurtured and guided me in this journey. Your example of unwavering devotion, godly counsel, and compassionate care has been a beacon of light and strength in my life. Thank you for standing as pillars of faith and for your steadfast commitment to the Kingdom

ACKNOWLEDGMENTS

This book would not have been possible without the unwavering support, dedication, and talent of an extraordinary team. My deepest gratitude goes to each of you for your contributions, insights, and encouragement throughout this journey.

First and foremost, thank you to Rev. Mimi Philemon my dear wife, Rev. Shina Gentry, and and my assistant pastor Rev. Bright Amudoaghan for your incredible effort, encouragement, and belief in this project. Your support has been instrumental in bringing this vision to life.

To the dedicated leaders of Royal Diadem Publishing, Ide Imogie and Kishawna Bailey, I am immensely grateful for your belief in this project from the very beginning and for investing your time and energy into its development. Your creativity, dedication, and expertise have been the backbone of this endeavor.

I am especially grateful to the Royal Diadem Publishing team— Beulah Orogun, Emmanuella Ben-Eboh, Doyinsade Awodele, Kim Matthews, and Shante Gill, for your meticulous attention to detail, refining every page and ensuring that each word reflects our vision.

A heartfelt thank you to my family, friends, and colleagues whose unwavering support and belief in this project gave me the courage and strength to see it through.

Finally, thank you to all the readers and supporters who make this work meaningful. I am humbled and honored to share this journey with each of you.

With all my gratitude,
David Philemon

CONTENTS

INTRODUCTION

THE STAGE IS SET

W elcome to Riding the High Waves, where life's storms are not just obstacles but opportunities for divine intervention and growth. Imagine life as a grand theater, where each of us plays a unique role in a dramatic unfolding story.

The stage is set, the script is already written, and the waves of life rise high, challenging us to step into our God-ordained roles with courage and faith.

In this journey through high waves, you will discover that these turbulent moments are not meant to drown you but to elevate you. Each storm you face is a scene in the divine drama, orchestrated by a loving and omnipotent Director who has scripted a victorious ending. The enemy may plot and scheme, attempting to destabilize and distract, but God's script is unchanging, and His purpose for your life is unshakable.

This book serves as your guide through these high waves. It reminds you that despite the chaos and confusion, God has already laid a path to triumph. As you navigate through the chapters, you'll uncover powerful principles and actionable insights designed to help you align with God's script, remain steadfast in the face of challenges, and harness His power to fulfill your divine purpose.

The high waves may be daunting, but remember: they are part of a grand narrative in which you are called to rise, stand firm, and embrace your role. Let Riding the *High Waves* be your compass, encouragement, and source of strength as you navigate through the storms and emerge victorious, anchored in the Word and unwavering promise of God's guidance and grace.

CHAPTER
ONE

When the waves rise high,
it's not a sign of your defeat
but of God's impending
display of Power.

APOSTLE DR. DAVID PHILEMON

CHAPTER ONE

THE DRAMA OF LIFE

L ife, as we know it, is often likened to a stage where each individual plays a role. The twists and turns of our existence are akin to the acts in a play, filled with moments of suspense, unexpected shifts, and climactic revelations. However, unlike a scripted play where the outcome is predetermined, our lives unfold in real-time, often bringing unforeseen challenges that test our faith and resilience. These challenges, symbolized by the high waves of life, are not mere obstacles meant to hinder us; they are divine setups for God to demonstrate His unparalleled power and faithfulness.

THE SUDDEN STORMS OF LIFE

Storms in life often arise without warning, catching us off guard and shaking the very foundations of our faith. Just as a sailor might find themselves in calm waters one moment and battling fierce waves the next, so too do we encounter unexpected difficulties that threaten to overwhelm us. These storms can manifest in financial crises, health issues, broken relationships, or even spiritual droughts. The suddenness of these storms can leave us feeling disoriented and vulnerable, questioning why we are facing such turbulence.

Unforeseen storms can present some of the toughest challenges we face. Unexpected and unpredicted storms can make us wonder if God controls our lives. Death, illness, job loss, fractured relationships, anxieties, and setbacks are among the challenges our enemy, Satan, may wield to engulf us in feelings of doubt. He understands that we tend to become more easily disheartened when stressed and tired. You might have encountered an unforeseen storm or be currently facing one. Several of the disciples had extensive experience in fishing. Peter and the other disciples, who were fishermen, typically fished at night, so embarking on a journey across the lake at sunset would not have seemed risky. Fishing was most successful in the evening, while storms on the Sea of Galilee typically happened in the afternoon. The disciples were surprised when a storm hit as they set out in their boat. Humans may believe we are resilient and in charge, but we often realize we are as delicate as eggshells. **James 4:14: You do not know what will happen tomorrow. Your life is like a cloud that appears for a short time and then quickly goes away. Easy English Bible.** Life changes when we emerge from the other side of a storm. We begin to perceive those around us in a different light and may even reevaluate our sense of purpose. Several people found their careers less significant after experiencing a health crisis. Life's uncertainties frequently prompt us to see what truly matters.

Unexpected life storms highlight our need to rely on Jesus. Although a storm may arise suddenly and without warning, our relationship with Jesus is the steady anchor we can always hold onto. A tumultuous period might sweep away many things, but it will never diminish our bond with Jesus. Regardless of how fiercely the storm may strike, our connection with Jesus will uphold and guide us to safety.

The disciples experienced a literal storm in the Bible while on the Sea of Galilee. They were seasoned fishermen familiar with the unpredictable nature of the sea, yet this storm was unlike any they had encountered before. As the waves crashed against their boat, they were filled with fear despite having Jesus with them.

37 Suddenly, as they crossed the lake, a ferocious storm arose,

with violent winds and waves crashing into the boat until it was nearly swamped.

38 But Jesus was calmly sleeping in the stern, resting on a cushion. So they shook him awake, saying, "Teacher, don't you even care that we are all about to die!"

39 Fully awake, he rebuked the storm and shouted to the sea, "Hush! Be still!" All at once, the wind stopped howling, and the water became perfectly calm.

40 Then he turned to his disciples and said, "Why are you so afraid? Haven't you learned to trust yet?"

~ MARK 4:37-40 TPT

This narrative powerfully illustrates how even those who walk closely with God are not exempt from the storms of life. It also highlights that these storms are not a sign of God's absence but rather an opportunity for Him to reveal His power in a new and profound way.

Jesus has power over the storms we face, even if this wasn't obvious initially. The disciples searched for Jesus on the ship, but they found Him sleeping on a cushion at the rear of the boat. In His human form, Jesus was asleep. However, when they awakened Him, He calmed the storm with His divine power! When the disciples noticed Jesus sleeping, they said to him. "Lord, aren't you concerned that we're about to drown in this storm?" Have you ever said something like that to the Lord? I think we all have at some point. We should keep in mind that our Lord always prioritizes our best interests. He looks out for us. In **1 Peter 5:7**, it is stated, **"If you have any kind of trouble in your mind, give it to God. God has promised to take care of you." Easy English Bible.**

Jesus was a comforting presence for them in the storm, although they initially didn't realize it. Can we be in such a severe storm that we fail to recognize how near Christ is? We must always maintain our faith. Don't allow situations to dictate your mindset or behavior. Rely on Jesus during your difficult times. When the disciples woke Jesus, He questioned why they let fear take over instead of relying on their faith. Jesus emphasized that you cannot simultaneously harbor fear and faith in your heart. You need to have either one or the other occupying the space. No matter the storm, Jesus is greater and more powerful. What we require is a faith strong enough to drive out fear.

Your life has a leader when Jesus is around.

A captain is responsible for overseeing a ship and provides guidance and orders to everyone on board. Jesus is the Commander of our salvation, fully aware of the perils we encounter on our journey. He has the ability to navigate us away from them, guide us through them, or help us rise above them. Recall the moment he walked on water during the storm? With Jesus as the helmsman of your life, you have a powerful leader guiding you.

Long ago, a ship was battered by a tempest. A man was feeling scared, but then he noticed a young boy who appeared completely at ease. Curious, he asked the child, "Son, how can you remain so calm during this terrible storm?" The boy answered, "My dad is the captain, and he has never lost a ship." Similarly, dear friend, Jesus is our Captain, and He has never lost anyone under His care —you can place your trust in Him.

Your life follows a path when Jesus is involved.

Without Jesus, your life resembles a ship adrift on the ocean, buffeted by waves and lacking direction. You wander without a goal or clear path. In today's message, He instructed His disciples to cross to the opposite shore. He was aware of the storm they were approaching, and he also understood that adhering to his guidance would not result in their downfall. Obeying the Lord's guidance may not guarantee an easy path, but it does ensure that you are choosing the best course of action.

Your life reaches fulfillment when Jesus is present.

Jesus will guide you to your final destination. In verse 35, Jesus informed His disciples that they were headed to the opposite shore. Having Jesus in your life guarantees that you will reach your destination safely. In **2 Timothy 1:12**, it says, **"That is why I have these troubles. But I am not ashamed to be in prison. I have believed in Christ and I know him well. I know that I can trust him to keep his message safe. God has given me the authority to speak that message to people at this time. Christ has the power to keep it safe until that great day when he comes back."** **Easy English Bible** Our protection does not come from our own strength; instead, it comes from God's power. He assures us that He will use His love and strength to guide us to the destination He has promised.

What does it mean to have faith? Faith means trusting God's promises. It's important to mention that Jesus had previously informed the disciples that they would cross to the other side. They were unable to drown after Jesus had assured them. However, they focused on the winds and waves, which made them overlook Jesus's promise. The risk for a believer is to let fear during a crisis overshadow their faith in the Savior. He has made a promise to us, assuring that He will always be with us and will never abandon us. Trust in what God says!

What Jesus accomplished was adequate. In verse 37, it mentions that a storm began. In verse 39, it mentions that Jesus got up. Thank God, when challenges come, Jesus will rise up in your life. When you find yourself in the midst of a storm, keep in mind as a Christian that Jesus is aboard the ship of your life alongside you. It's terrifying to find yourself in a dangerous storm without a companion. Keep this in mind: finding safety during a storm doesn't mean the storm isn't there; rather, true safety comes from having Jesus with you in the midst of it. Nothing can go wrong with Jesus on board. Jesus was not only with them during the storm, but He also had authority over it. If Jesus doesn't rescue you from the storm, He will guide you through it. If He doesn't bring tranquility to your surroundings, He will bring peace to your heart. No matter what He does, He always supports those who have embraced Him and place their complete trust in Him.

A Case Study: The Israelites At The Red Sea

One of the most dramatic moments in the Bible is the account of the Israelites at the Red Sea. After being freed from the bondage of Egypt, the Israelites found themselves in a seemingly impossible situation. With Pharaoh's army pursuing them from behind and the Red Sea blocking their path forward, they were trapped with no apparent way out. This moment of impending doom was a test of their faith and trust in God's promise of deliverance.

8 He pursued the people of Israel, for they had taken much of the wealth of Egypt with them.

9 Pharaoh's entire cavalry—horses, chariots, and charioteers— was used in the chase; and the Egyptian army overtook the people of Israel as they were camped beside the shore near Piha- hiroth, across from Baal-zephon.

10 As the Egyptian army approached, the people of Israel saw them far in the distance, speeding after them, and they were terribly frightened and cried out to the Lord to help them.

11 And they turned against Moses, whining, "Have you brought us out here to die in the desert because there were not enough graves for us in Egypt? Why did you make us leave Egypt?

12 Isn't this what we told you, while we were enslaved, to leave us alone? We said it would be better to be slaves to the Egyptians than dead in the wilderness.

~ EXODUS 14:8-12TLB

From a human perspective, their situation was hopeless. They were not equipped to fight the well-trained Egyptian army, nor did they have the means to cross the vast sea before them. In that moment of despair, they cried out to Moses, questioning why they had been brought to the wilderness only to die. But what they perceived as their end was, in fact, the perfect setup for a divine intervention.

God's response to their cries was not to scold them for their lack of faith, but to instruct Moses to lift his staff and stretch out his hand over the sea. What happened next was nothing short of miraculous. The Red Sea parted, creating a dry path for the Israelites to cross safely to the other side. As the Egyptians pursued them, the waters closed back in, drowning Pharaoh's entire army. What seemed like an insurmountable challenge was transformed into a moment of triumph, showcasing God's power and faithfulness.

21   Meanwhile, Moses stretched his rod over the sea, and the Lord opened up a path through the sea, with walls of water on each side; and a strong east wind blew all that night, drying the sea bottom.

22 So the people of Israel walked through the sea on dry ground!

23   Then the Egyptians followed them between the walls of water along the bottom of the sea—all of Pharaoh's horses, chariots, and horsemen.

~ EXODUS 14:21-23 TLB

This story serves as a powerful reminder that when we are on the brink of despair, feeling cornered by life's circumstances, God is often preparing to act in a way that exceeds our expectations. The key lies in our ability to trust Him, even when the waves are high and the situation appears dire.

TRUSTING GOD AMID HIGH WAVES

Trust is a fundamental aspect of our relationship with God, particularly when we face the high waves of life. It is easy to trust

God when things are going well, but true faith is tested amid adversity. When we encounter storms, our natural inclination is often to panic, to look for a way out, or to try to take control of the situation ourselves. However, these responses can lead to further turmoil, as we become overwhelmed by the magnitude of the problem.

The story of the Israelites at the Red Sea teaches us that the key to overcoming the high waves of life is to place our trust entirely in God. This trust is not passive; it requires active faith—believing that God is who He says He is and that He will do what He has promised, even when the circumstances suggest otherwise. It is the kind of trust that says, "I may not see the way out, but I know that God will make a way."

In the New Testament, the Apostle Peter provides another example of the importance of keeping our eyes on Jesus amid life's storms. When Peter saw Jesus walking on water, he asked to join Him. Jesus invited Peter to step out of the boat, and Peter began walking on the water toward Him. However, as soon as Peter took his eyes off Jesus and focused on the wind and waves around him, he began to sink. Jesus immediately reached out and caught him, asking, "Why did you doubt?"

29-30 He said, "Come ahead."

Jumping out of the boat, Peter walked on the water to Jesus. But when he looked down at the waves churning beneath his feet, he lost his nerve and started to sink. He cried, "Master, save me!"

31 Jesus didn't hesitate. He reached down and grabbed his hand. Then he said, "Faint heart, what got into you?"

~ MATTHEW 14:31 MSG

Peter's experience illustrates the danger of allowing our focus to shift from Jesus to the problems around us. When we concentrate on the high waves, we become consumed by fear and doubt, causing us to sink into despair. But when we keep our eyes on Jesus, trusting in His ability to calm the storm, we find the strength to walk above the waves.

We've all experienced that moment, caught in the chaos as the waters rise, pondering how we arrived at this point. Where is God amid the storm? When I'm exhausted and my spirit is worn down, when life has taken so much from me that I'm left gasping from its harshness. When life's storms arise, they take away our tranquility. It is during the height of a storm, as the floodwaters rise and loom over us, that we need to choose whether we will let God work through this difficult situation. To be the one who governs both the storms and the joyful moments in our lives. Or let the tumultuous times break our trust and lead us away from God's love. In difficult moments and sorrow, it's easy to let the turmoil turn us resentful and distance us from the plans God has for us, causing us to lose sight of His teachings and the perfect peace He offers. Ultimately, this is a decision we need to make during the fierce winds and chaotic storm that we are currently experiencing or will experience in the future.

Life's challenges can serve as a means of refinement and growth, and one day, God will restore this fractured world. Alternatively, it can arrive suddenly like a tornado, leaving destruction in its wake. It may seem daunting to have faith in God when you're facing a crisis that He was aware of but chose not to shield you from. Why, with all of God's strength, did He permit this day of hardship? What is difficult to understand right now, from our viewpoint, is the reason we had to go through the storm. Believe me, I've faced my fair share of challenges and have had countless sleepless nights crying into my pillow, questioning God about it all. I can assure you, without any doubt, that there is always a purpose behind it. Some of the most intense storms I've faced have served as opportunities for God to make His presence known in a significant way. And shower all of His grace, compassion, and affection upon the life of another soul weathered by storms. At times, we must weather the storm to remove the dependencies we have, allowing us to encounter God during us the turmoil.

How to Have Faith in God during Difficult Times

Even with the awareness that He is God amidst the storm, doubts can still arise when we confront the challenges the storm presents. How can you maintain your faith in God during difficult times?

- Worship God during the storms. Even when you're not in the mood. Even when we don't feel like it, one of the greatest offerings we can present to God is the gift of praise. When our lives are falling apart, this specific task helps us focus on our mighty God rather than the chaos surrounding us.

- Share your innermost feelings with your Father. He is already aware of your emotions and the thoughts in your mind, so go ahead and express them. It's perfectly normal to feel angry, to experience pain, and to seek answers. Provided that these issues don't develop into resentment that hinders your relationship with God.

- Entrust it to God—the challenges we encounter can be overwhelming and burdensome for us to handle alone, and that was never our intention. Place your burdens down at His feet. God's plans aren't our plans, so we frequently encounter unexpected situations. It's essential to entrust these times to God and maintain faith that He has a purpose for us.

- During turbulent times, it can be challenging to hold onto the promises we've gathered during happier moments. However, the storm frequently reinforces the lessons we learned when everything was going smoothly. The reality is that we require the storms. Although these periods in your life may be uncomfortable and painful, they help us grow and develop. They remove the superficial layers and compel us to deepen our trust in Christ Jesus.

GOD'S POWER REVEALED IN OUR WEAKNESS

One of the most profound truths in the Christian faith is that God's power is made perfect in our weakness. The Apostle Paul writes in 2 Corinthians 12:9,

'But he answered me, "My grace is always more than enough for you, and my power finds its full expression through your weakness." So I will celebrate my weaknesses, for when I'm weak I sense more deeply the mighty power of Christ living in me.'

~ 2 CORINTHIANS 12:9 TPT

This means that it is often in our most vulnerable and desperate moments that God chooses to display His strength and glory.

The high waves of life have a way of stripping us of our illusions of control and self-sufficiency. They bring us to the end of ourselves, where we must acknowledge our need for God's intervention. It is in these moments of surrender that God steps in, turning what seems like a hopeless situation into a testimony of His faithfulness.

The Israelites' experience at the Red Sea is a prime example of this principle. Their weakness was evident—they had no military strength, no strategic plan, and no natural way to escape their predicament. Yet, it was precisely in this moment of weakness that God demonstrated His unmatched power. The parting of the Red Sea was not just a miraculous escape; it was a revelation of God's sovereignty over all creation, His ability to make a way where there seems to be no way.

Similarly, in our lives, God often allows us to face situations that are beyond our ability to handle so that we can experience His power more deeply. These high waves are not meant to destroy us, but to build our faith and draw us closer to Him. They are opportunities for us to witness the greatness of God and to grow in our trust and dependence on Him.

THE DRAMA OF LIFE: A DIVINE SETUP

As we journey through life, we will inevitably encounter moments of drama—times when the waves seem too high and the storm too fierce. But as believers, we can take comfort in knowing that these moments are not random or meaningless. They are divine setups, orchestrated by God to bring about His purposes in our lives.

The drama of life is part of God's grand narrative, in which He is both the Author and the Director. He knows the beginning from the end, and He has already written the script. While we may not always understand why certain things happen, we can trust that God is in control and that He is working all things together for our good.

"So we are convinced that every detail of our lives is continually woven together for good, for we are his lovers who have been called to fulfill his designed purpose."

~ ROMANS 8:28 TPT

In the face of life's high waves, our response should not be one of fear or despair, but of faith and expectation. We should look to God with anticipation, knowing that He is about to do something extraordinary. Just as He parted the Red Sea for the Israelites and calmed the storm for the disciples, He will act on our behalf in ways that will leave us in awe of His power and goodness.

CHAPTER TWO

The true strength lies not in bargaining with God, but in surrendering completely to His perfect plan.

APOSTLE DR. DAVID PHILEMON

CHAPTER TWO

CUTTING DEALS
WITH GOD

Humans tend to negotiate. In the course of our spiritual journeys, we often find ourselves at a crossroads where we are tempted to negotiate with God. This negotiation usually takes the form of conditional promises: "God, if You do this for me, then I will do that for You." It's a reflection of our human nature, deeply ingrained in us from a young age. We negotiate in our daily lives—whether bargaining for a better price, negotiating terms in a contract, or compromising in relationships. This behavior often extends to our relationship with God, where we try to barter our obedience in exchange for blessings.

This tendency to negotiate stems from a desire to maintain control. We want to feel that we have some influence over the outcomes in our lives. By offering God something—our obedience, time, and sacrifices—we hope to secure the desired results. However, this approach reveals a fundamental misunderstanding of the nature of our relationship with God. God is not a business partner with whom we can strike a deal; He is our Creator, Lord, and Father, who desires total surrender and trust.

The Flawed Nature Of Our Bargains

When we attempt to cut deals with God, we often do so with flawed motives. Our focus is on the blessings we hope to receive rather than on deepening our relationship with Him. We may offer our obedience, but it is often conditional and incomplete. We may commit to spending more time in prayer, attending church more regularly, or giving more generously, but these commitments are made with the expectation of receiving something in return.

This transactional approach to faith is contrary to the nature of God's love and grace. God's blessings are not for sale, nor are they given as a reward for good behavior. They are expressions of His unmerited favor and love for us. When we attempt to earn His blessings through our deeds, we reduce our relationship with Him to a mere exchange, missing out on the depth and richness of His grace.

The Danger Of Losing Focus: Peter's Example

The story of Peter walking on water, found in Matthew 14:29-30, provides a powerful illustration of the perils of trying to negotiate with God and the importance of maintaining our focus on Him. When Jesus called Peter to leave the boat and walk on water, Peter responded with faith and courage. As long as he kept his eyes on Jesus, he could do the impossible—he walked on the water toward his Lord.

However, the moment Peter shifted his focus from Jesus to the wind and the waves around him, he began to sink. His fear and doubt overwhelmed him, and he cried out to Jesus to save him. This story highlights the critical importance of where we place our focus. When Peter focused on Jesus, he could transcend the natural laws of physics. But when he allowed the circumstances around him to distract him, he was quickly overcome by his fears.

Like Peter, when we try to cut deals with God, we are often more focused on the "waves" around us—the challenges, uncertainties, and fears—than on Jesus. We seek to secure our safety and comfort through negotiation, rather than trusting fully in God's power and love. But, as Peter's experience teaches us, when we lose sight of Jesus and allow our fears to dictate our actions, we are likely to sink into the depths of our doubts.

Surrendering To God's Will

The concept of surrender is central to the Christian faith. Surrendering to God means relinquishing control and trusting Him with every aspect of our lives. It is a recognition that His ways are higher than ours, and His thoughts are higher than our thoughts (Isaiah 55:9).

"For just as the heavens are higher than the earth, so are my ways higher than yours, and my thoughts than yours."

~ ISAIAH 55:9 TLB

God's plans for us are perfect, even when we cannot see the full picture.

Surrender is not a one-time event but a daily decision. It requires us to continually trust God, even when circumstances are difficult or the outcomes are uncertain. True surrender means saying, "Not my will, but Yours be done," just as Jesus did in the Garden of Gethsemane (Luke 22:42).

"Father, if you are willing, take this cup of agony away from me. But no matter what, your will must be mine."

~ LUKE 22:42 TPT

It is a declaration of faith that God's plan is good and the best possible outcome for our lives.

We release the need to negotiate or bargain when we surrender to God. We trust that He knows what is best for us, and we rest in the assurance that He is in control. This surrender does not mean passivity; rather, it involves actively aligning our will with God's, seeking to live in obedience to His Word and guidance.

Many Christians find it difficult to follow God's will and have faith in His guidance because they lack a clear understanding of true surrender. Ultimately, yielding to God is not the same as giving in due to defeat. In this situation, you express to God that you prefer His wishes. You acknowledge that you feel incapable of guiding your own life and would rather have Him take control. Surrendering everything to God means giving up your control, plans, and understanding to Him. You begin to resemble a sheep guided by its shepherd, as He guides your paths, choices, and structures your life. Doesn't it seem like you are surrendering your will and acting foolishly? While it may appear that way to a conventional mindset, for those who are spiritually enlightened, it's actually the best choice you can make, as it's when you truly start to live.

Jesus Christ serves as the ideal model in this context. Just hours before His arrest and crucifixion, He expressed, "Not my will, but yours." Though He wished for the burden to be lifted from Him, He ultimately submitted to the will of the Father. If it required Him to sacrifice His life, then so be it.

The Freedom In Surrender

Surrendering to God brings profound freedom. When we let go of our attempts to control or negotiate our way through life, we find peace in the knowledge that God is sovereign. We no longer have to carry the burden of trying to manipulate outcomes or secure blessings through our efforts. Instead, we can rest in God's promises, knowing that He is faithful and that His love for us is unconditional.

This freedom allows us to live with an open heart, ready to receive whatever God has in store for us. It enables us to face challenges with confidence, knowing that God is with us and that He is working all things together for our good. **Romans 8:28 We know that God works to help those people who love him. He uses**

everything that happens to them to bring something good. He does this for those people that he has chosen to serve him. *Easy English Bible*

Surrendering to God also deepens our relationship with Him, as we learn to trust Him more fully and to rely on His strength rather than our own.

Trusting In God's Perfect Plan

One of the most significant challenges in surrendering to God is trusting His timing and plan. God's ways are often mysterious, and His timing can be difficult to understand. We may find ourselves in situations where we are tempted to take matters into our own hands, to try to force a solution, or to negotiate a different outcome.

However, trusting in God's plan means believing that He has already written the script for our lives and that it is perfect. Even when we cannot see the end from the beginning, we can trust that God is leading us on the right path. This trust is rooted in the knowledge that God is good, that He loves us, and that He is always working for our ultimate good.

In times of uncertainty or difficulty, this trust becomes our anchor. It keeps us grounded in the truth of God's Word and prevents us from being tossed about by the waves of doubt and fear. By trusting in God's plan, we can face life's challenges with courage and confidence, knowing He is with us every step.

Moving Beyond Deals To A Relationship Of Trust

The call of the Christian life is not to a series of negotiations with God but to a relationship of trust and love. God is not interested in our attempts to bargain with Him; He desires our hearts. He wants us to know Him, to love Him, and to trust Him completely.

When we move beyond cutting deals with God, we enter into a deeper, more intimate relationship with Him. This relationship is characterized by trust, surrender, and a deep sense of peace. It is a relationship in which we learn to listen to God's voice, to follow His leading, and to rest in His love.

This relationship also transforms our understanding of obedience. Rather than seeing obedience as a means to an end, we see it as a joyful response to God's love. We obey not because we are trying to earn something from God, but because we love Him and trust Him. Our obedience becomes an act of worship, a way of expressing our love and gratitude to the One who has given us everything.

The Call To Trust And Surrender

Cutting deals with God may seem like a natural response to life's challenges and uncertainties, but it is ultimately a futile endeavor. God is not interested in our negotiations; He desires our total surrender and trust. Like Peter, we are called to keep our eyes on Jesus, to trust in His power, and to walk in faith, even when the waves around us seem overwhelming.

As we learn to trust in God's plan and surrender our will to His, we will discover the freedom and peace that comes from living in alignment with His purposes. We will move beyond a transactional relationship with God to a deep, abiding relationship of trust and love. In this relationship, we will find the strength, courage, and joy we need to navigate the high waves of life.

Ways To Fully Submit To God

The Bible encourages us to devote our lives to God in various passages. Having grasped the concept of true surrender, we now ask, "What does it mean to fully surrender to God?" The reality is that there isn't a definite method for this, as surrendering is an ongoing journey. Here are some suggestions for ways to fully surrender to God each day:

Prayer is crucial

Prayer isn't merely a way to convey our needs to God; it's a moment of connection and communion with Him. The more time you dedicate to prayer, the simpler it becomes to submit to Him. Why is this? Prayer helps you concentrate on God and His character. It shows you different aspects of God, leading to a shift in your perspective. Through prayer, you develop a greater dependency on God, and He starts to show you His intentions and plans for your life.

Practice waiting on God

Waiting is one of the toughest tasks, particularly in today's context. Humans are constantly in motion. We are eager to set our plans in motion. Sometimes, the most effective way to fully entrust everything to God is by practicing patience. Have you found yourself praying without receiving a clear response? Or perhaps you've been examining a section of scripture but still lack guidance? In such moments, you may be in a season where God asks you to be patient and wait. As you wait for Him, it's important to keep praying and studying; sometimes, you might also consider fasting. The positive aspect is that the "wait" is always worthwhile **Isaiah 40:31, But people who wait for the Lord to help them will receive new strength. They will rise up high, as if they have the wings of eagles. They will run, and they will not become tired. They will walk, and they will not become weak.** *Easy English Bible*

Bible Study

It might seem trite, but the Bible offers guidance and teachings to assist us in following God's will. Various sections of the scripture highlight this truth. One of God's initial directives to Joshua, as he assumed leadership from Moses, was to remain committed to the Word. The Psalmist emphasizes this point by describing God's Word as a guiding light for his journey. Exploring the Scriptures allows you to understand God's plan for your life. It also helps you determine whether your choices and plans are in harmony with God's intentions. When you read the Bible with the guidance of the Holy Spirit, you'll frequently receive clear insights. Giving everything to God is easier than you might believe. When you grasp its true meaning and successfully implement it, you gain significant rewards.

CHAPTER
THREE

The enemy's fiercest
attacks often signal the
birth of
God's greatest plans.

APOSTLE DR. DAVID PHILEMON

CHAPTER THREE

THE ENEMY'S STRATEGY

In the grand drama of life, we must recognize that we are not the only ones with a plan. The enemy, too, is crafting strategies, working tirelessly to derail God's purposes. His methods are often subtle, disguised in distractions, divisions, and discouragements, designed to weaken our resolve and draw us away from the path God has set before us. To navigate these high waves of spiritual warfare, we must be vigilant, unified, and anchored in our faith, for the enemy's strategy is both insidious and relentless.

THE SUBTLETY OF DISTRACTION

The enemy's first line of attack often comes in the form of distraction. In a world filled with endless noise and countless demands on our attention, it is easy to lose focus on what truly matters. The enemy knows that a distracted believer is a vulnerable believer. By diverting our attention from God's voice, the enemy seeks to weaken our spiritual awareness, making us susceptible to his influence.

Consider how often our days are filled with activities that, while not inherently sinful, serve to draw us away from time in presence. The busyness of life, the allure of entertainment, and even the pressures of work can become distractions that erode our spiritual vitality. In these moments, the enemy is not merely content to pull us away from prayer or Bible study; he aims to gradually dull our sensitivity to the Holy Spirit's leading.

In the parable of the sower, Jesus warned of the seed that fell among thorns, which represents those who hear the word, but "the worries of this life, the deceitfulness of wealth, and the desires for other things come in and choke the word, making it unfruitful" (NIV).

18 The thorny ground represents the hearts of people who listen to the Good News and receive it,

19 but all too quickly the attractions of this world and the delights of wealth, and the search for success and lure of nice things come in and crowd out God's message from their hearts so that no crop is produced.

~ MARK 4:18-19TLB

The enemy's strategy is to choke the life out of our spiritual walk, not through outright sin, but through the slow, subtle distractions that distance us from God.

To counter this, we must cultivate a disciplined life of focus and intention. Like the apostle Paul, we must "press on toward the goal to win the prize for which God has called [us] heavenward in Christ Jesus" (Philippians 3:14, NIV). This requires setting boundaries, prioritizing time with God, and being mindful of how the enemy seeks to distract us from our divine purpose.

The Danger Of Division

If distraction is the enemy's subtle strategy, division is his more overt and devastating weapon. The enemy knows that a house divided against itself cannot stand.

No kingdom can endure if it is divided against itself, and a

fragmented household will not be able to stand, for it is divided.

~ MARK 3:25 TPT

In the body of Christ, division weakens our collective strength and compromises our witness to the world. The early church understood the importance of unity, as seen in Acts 2:44-47, where *"all the believers were together and had everything in common... They broke bread in their homes and ate together with glad and sincere hearts."*

Yet, the enemy constantly seeks to sow seeds of discord within the Church. Whether through doctrinal disagreements, personal conflicts, or cultural differences, the enemy's goal is to fracture the unity that Christ prayed for in John 17:21,

"My prayer for all of them is that they will be of one heart and mind, just as you and I are, Father—that just as you are in me and I am in you, so they will be in us, and the world will believe you sent me."

~ JOHN 17:21 TLB

The division does not only weaken the Church; it also hinders our ability to fulfill the Great Commission. When believers are at odds with one another, our focus shifts from advancing God's kingdom to defending our personal preferences and opinions. The enemy revels in this, knowing that a divided Church is an ineffective Church.

To overcome the enemy's strategy of division, we must be committed to unity in Christ. This means valuing relationships over being right, seeking reconciliation over retaliation, and prioritizing the mission of the Church over personal agendas. As Paul exhorted the Ephesian believers, we must *"make every effort to keep the unity of the Spirit through the bond of peace"* (Ephesians 4:3, NIV). Unity is not the absence of conflict, but the presence of a shared commitment to Christ and His purposes.

The Trap Of Discouragement

When distraction and division fail, the enemy often resorts to discouragement. He knows that a discouraged believer is one step away from giving up.

Discouragement can arise from unmet expectations, prolonged trials, or perceived failures. The enemy amplifies these feelings, whispering lies that God has forgotten us, that our efforts are in vain, or that we are unworthy of God's love and grace.

In the book of Nehemiah, we see how the enemy used discouragement as a tactic to stop the rebuilding of Jerusalem's walls. Sanballat, Tobiah, and others mocked and ridiculed the Israelites, hoping to demoralize them and halt their work. But Nehemiah's response was one of prayer and perseverance: *"Don't be afraid of them. Remember the Lord, who is great and awesome, and fight for your families, your sons and your daughters, your wives, and your homes"* (Nehemiah 4:14, NIV).

The enemy's goal is to make us lose heart, but God's strategy is to strengthen us through His word and presence. When we feel discouraged, we must turn to Scripture, where we find countless reminders of God's faithfulness. David, often surrounded by enemies and overwhelmed by trials, encouraged himself in the Lord.

"David was seriously worried, for in their bitter grief for their children, his men began talking of killing him. But David took strength from the Lord."

~ 1 SAMUEL 30:6 TLB

We must also learn to find our encouragement in God's promises, knowing He is with us and will never forsake us.

"Don't be obsessed with getting more material things. Be relaxed with what you have".

~ HEBREWS 13:5 MSG

The Need For Vigilance

In light of the enemy's strategies, the gatekeepers of the Church —the leaders, intercessors, and guards—must remain vigilant. Vigilance involves being spiritually alert, discerning the enemy's tactics, and responding with prayer and action. Jesus warned His disciples to *"watch and pray so that you will not fall into temptation. The spirit is willing, but the flesh is weak"* (Matthew 26:41, NIV). Vigilance is not just about avoiding sin; it's about staying attuned to the spiritual realities and being prepared to counter the enemy's advances.

The Apostle Peter, who knew firsthand the cost of letting down his guard, exhorted believers to *"be alert and of sober mind. Your enemy, the devil, prowls around like a roaring lion looking for someone to devour. Resist him, standing firm in the faith"* (NIV).

"Be well balanced and always alert because your enemy, the devil, roams around incessantly, like a roaring lion looking for its prey to devour."

~ 1 PETER5:8-9 TPT

The enemy's strategy is to catch us off guard, to find us unprepared and vulnerable. But when we are vigilant, rooted in God's word, and covered in prayer, we can stand firm against his attacks.

The Power Of Unity And Faith

Finally, the power to overcome the enemy's strategy lies in our unity and steadfast faith. The Church is most vital when we stand together, united in purpose and unwavering in our commitment to Christ. The early Church faced intense persecution, yet they *"raised their voices together in prayer to God"* (NIV), resulting in a mighty outpouring of the Holy Spirit.

'When the believers heard their report, they raised their voices in unity and prayed,

"Lord YAHWEH, you are the Lord of all! You created the universe —the earth, the sky, the sea, and everything that is in them." '

~ ACTS 4:24 TPT

When we unite in faith, the enemy's strategies are rendered ineffective. We become like the threefold cord that is not easily broken (Ecclesiastes 4:12). Our unity terrifies the enemy because it reflects the very nature of God—Father, Son, and Holy Spirit, three in one. In this unity, we find the strength to resist the enemy and advance God's kingdom.

Moreover, our faith in God's protection and provision shields us from the enemy's attacks. In Ephesians 6:16, Paul describes faith as a shield *"with which you can extinguish all the flaming arrows of the evil one."* Faith is our defense against the enemy's lies, discouragements, and temptations. Faith enables us to walk on water, move mountains, and stand firm in adversity.

Aligning With God's Strategy

In this ongoing spiritual battle, we must align ourselves with God's strategy grounded in truth, love, and righteousness. The enemy's strategy may be dramatic, but it is ultimately futile against the power of God. As we remain vigilant, united, and steadfast in the faith, we will see God's plans for our lives unfold, protect, and prosper by His hand.

CHAPTER
FOUR

A heart void of gratitude is
fertile ground for
deeper troubles.

APOSTLE DR. DAVID PHILEMON

CHAPTER FOUR

UNGRATEFULNESS AND ITS CONSEQUENCES

G ratitude is a powerful force in life and, ultimately, in our walk with God. It is more than a fleeting emotion; it is a foundational attitude that shapes our perception of life and our relationship with God. In the grand narrative of "The High Waves," gratitude is an anchor, stabilizing us amid the tumultuous challenges that life inevitably presents. When we cultivate a heart of gratitude, we not only recognize God's goodness but also empower ourselves to navigate the high waves with resilience and confidence.

Conversely, ungratefulness acts as a poison, undermining our faith and obscuring our vision of God's benevolence. This chapter delves into the destructive nature of ingratitude, its biblical manifestations, and the transformative power of gratitude in our spiritual journey.

The Nature Of Ungratefulness

Ungratefulness, or ingratitude, is a condition where we fail to acknowledge and appreciate the blessings and mercies bestowed upon us. It is a state of discontentment that breeds dissatisfaction, even in the face of abundant blessings. The human heart is prone to forgetfulness, especially when confronted with adversity. In such moments, our natural tendency is to focus on what we lack rather than what we have received.

Ingratitude is not merely an absence of gratitude but an active resistance against recognizing God's hand in our lives. It reflects a lack of trust and an inability to see beyond our immediate circumstances to God's greater purpose for us. This attitude can have profound spiritual and emotional consequences, weakening our connection with God and diminishing our capacity to endure life's storms.

The Israelites' Ingratitude

One of the Bible's most poignant illustrations of ungratefulness is found in the history of the Israelites. Despite witnessing countless miracles and experiencing God's unwavering faithfulness, the Israelites frequently forgot His goodness and grumbled against Him.

EXODUS AND THE WILDERNESS WANDERINGS

The Exodus narrative is replete with instances of the Israelites' ingratitude. After being delivered from slavery in Egypt through miraculous signs and wonders, they soon began to grumble about their circumstances. In Exodus, shortly after crossing the Red Sea, the people complained about the lack of water, questioning why Moses had brought them into the desert to die.

'Then the people turned against Moses. "Must we die of thirst?" they demanded.'

~ EXODUS 15:24 TLB

Similarly, in Numbers 14:1-4, after hearing the reports of the spies sent to Canaan, the Israelites expressed a desire to return to Egypt, distrusting God's promises. Their ingratitude led to a prolonged period of wandering in the wilderness due to their lack of faith and continual complaining.

Alament Of Israel'singratitude

Psalm 106:21-25 captures the essence of the Israelites' repeated ungratefulness:

21-22 Thus, they despised their Savior who had done such mighty miracles in Egypt and at the Red Sea.

23 So the Lord declared he would destroy them. But Moses, his chosen one, stepped into the breach between the people and their God and begged him to turn from his wrath and not destroy them.

24 They refused to enter the Promised Land, for they wouldn't believe his solemn oath to care for them.

25 Instead, they pouted in their tents and mourned and despised his command.

~ THE LIVING BIBLE (TLB)

This passage underscores the severity of their ingratitude. Despite God's provision and deliverance, the Israelites turned to idolatry and immoral practices, leading to dire consequences for themselves and the land they inhabited.

Consequences Of Ingratitude

The Israelites' ungratefulness resulted in prolonged hardship and suffering. Their persistent grumbling and lack of faith meant that God allowed them to wander the wilderness for forty years, denying them the Promised Land. This extended period was not just a punishment but a transformative journey meant to purify their faith and prepare them for future responsibilities.

Ingratitude erodes trust, fosters disobedience, and invites divine discipline. The Israelites' examples serve as a cautionary tale for believers today, highlighting the importance of maintaining a grateful heart even in times of trial.

The Consequences Of Ingratitude

Ungratefulness carries significant spiritual, emotional, and relational consequences. When we fail to recognize and appreciate blessings, we open ourselves to various forms of spiritual decay and personal discontent.

Spiritual Consequences

Weakened Faith: Ingratitude diminishes our faith by causing us to question God's goodness and His intentions for our lives. When we focus on what we lack, we begin to doubt God's provision and sovereignty.

Reduced Spiritual Sensitivity: A heart burdened with ingratitude becomes less receptive to the Holy

Spirit's guidance. We become desensitized to God's presence and His ongoing work in our lives.

Increased Sinfulness: Ingratitude can lead to sinful behaviors as we seek fulfillment and satisfaction in things apart from God. It can manifest in idolatry, materialism, and other forms of disobedience.

Emotional Consequences

Chronic Discontentment: Ungratefulness fosters a perpetual dissatisfaction, making it difficult to experience joy and peace. We become trapped in a cycle of longing for more, never finding contentment in our current blessings.

Anxiety and Stress: Focusing on what we lack rather than what we have can heighten anxiety and stress. It creates a sense of scarcity and fear about the future.

Bitterness and Resentment: Ingratitude can breed bitterness towards God and others, damaging our relationships and overall emotional well-being.

Relational Consequences

Strained Relationships: A lack of gratitude can lead to selfishness and a lack of appreciation for others, straining personal and communal relationships.

Isolation: Ungratefulness can isolate us from the community of believers, as we fail to contribute positively to the body of Christ and may push others away with our negative attitudes.

Compromised Witness: When we exhibit ingratitude, it can negatively impact our witness to the world. Others may perceive us as unthankful and unsatisfied, which can hinder our ability to share God's love effectively.

Gratitude As A Weapon Against High Waves

In the face of life's high waves, gratitude is a powerful weapon that counters the effects of ungratefulness. It shifts our focus from our problems to God's provision, fostering a spirit of contentment and resilience.

Gratitude redirects our attention to what God has done rather than what we lack. It shifts our focus to God's goodness. Acknowledging His blessings reinforces our trust in His faithfulness and sovereignty. This perspective shift helps us remain steadfast amid trials, knowing that God is in control and working all things for our good (Romans 8:28).

A grateful heart is fortified against despair and hopelessness. Gratitude systematically builds resilience and strength. When we recognize God's past faithfulness, we are more equipped to confidently handle present challenges. Gratitude builds spiritual resilience, enabling us to withstand the high waves without being overwhelmed.

Expressing gratitude deepens and enhances our relationship with God. It fosters a sense of intimacy and dependence as we acknowledge that everything we have is a gift from Him. This acknowledgment cultivates a humble spirit, open to receiving more of His grace and guidance.

Gratitude is contagious. When we express thankfulness, we encourage and inspire others to recognize and appreciate God's blessings in their own lives. This mutual encouragement strengthens the community of believers, creating a supportive environment where faith can flourish.

Cultivating A Grateful Heart

Cultivating gratitude is a deliberate process that involves several spiritual disciplines and mindset shifts. Recognizing and appreciating God's work in our lives requires a conscious effort, even amid difficulties.

Taking time each day to reflect on God's blessings helps to foster a habit of gratitude. This can be done through journaling, prayer, or simply meditating on God's goodness. By recounting the ways God has provided and protected us, we train our hearts to focus on His faithfulness.

Contentment is a key component of gratitude. Learning and practicing to be content with what we have, rather than constantly striving for more, helps to curb feelings of envy and dissatisfaction. Philippians 4:11-13 encourages believers to find contentment in all circumstances through Christ who strengthens us.

11   Not that I was ever in need, for I have learned how to get along happily whether I have much or little.

12   I know how to live on almost nothing or with everything. I have learned the secret of contentment in every situation, whether it be a full stomach or hunger, plenty or want;

13 for I can do everything God asks me to with the help of Christ who gives me the strength and power.

~ PHILIPPIANS 4:11-13TLB

Serving others shifts our focus from our own needs to the needs of those around us. Acts of service foster a sense of gratitude by reminding us of the blessings we have received and encouraging us to share those blessings with others.

Scripture is a powerful tool for cultivating gratitude. Verses that highlight God's provision, faithfulness, and love can serve as reminders to be thankful. Psalms, in particular, are filled with expressions of gratitude and praise.

Keeping a gratitude journal is a practical way to track and reflect on the blessings in our lives. Writing down daily blessings, no matter how small, reinforces a thankful mindset and provides encouragement during challenging times.

Surrounding ourselves with people who practice gratitude can influence our attitudes. A community that encourages thankfulness creates an environment where gratitude thrives and becomes a shared value.

Worship is an act of gratitude. We express our thankfulness to God through singing, prayer, and other forms of worship. Regular participation in worship helps to keep our hearts attuned to God's goodness and fosters a spirit of gratitude.

Practical Steps To Develop Gratitude

Developing gratitude requires intentional practices that help us recognize and appreciate God's blessings. Here are some practical steps to cultivate a grateful heart:

Start and End Your Day with Gratitude

Begin each day by thanking God for a new day and its

opportunities. End your day by reflecting on the blessings and moments of joy you experienced. This routine frames your day with a focus on gratitude.

Create a Gratitude List

Maintain a list of things you are grateful for. Whenever you feel overwhelmed or disheartened, refer to this list to remind yourself of God's goodness.

Express Gratitude to Others

Take time to thank those around you. Expressing gratitude to others encourages them and reinforces your sense of thankfulness.

Meditate on God's Promises

Spend time meditating on promises from God's Word that affirm His faithfulness and provision. Let these promises anchor your heart in gratitude.

Limit Negative Influences

Identify and minimize sources of negativity that foster ingratitude, such as certain media, environments, or relationships. Surround yourself with positive influences that promote thankfulness.

Practice Mindfulness

Be present in each moment and recognize God's small blessings daily. Mindfulness helps to heighten your awareness of God's continuous presence and provision.

Engage in Acts of Kindness

Performing acts of kindness for others can increase your awareness of the blessings in your own life. Helping others fosters a sense of gratitude by shifting your focus outward.

Reflect on Past Blessings

Regularly take time to remember and recount the ways God has blessed you in the past. This reflection strengthens your faith and gratitude for His ongoing work.

The Role Of Gratitude In Spiritual

GROWTH

Gratitude is integral to spiritual growth, catalyzing deeper faith and a more intimate relationship with God. When we practice gratitude, we align ourselves with God's heart and open ourselves to His transformative work.

Enhancing Faith and Trust

Gratitude reinforces our trust in God's provision and care. As we acknowledge His blessings, our faith is strengthened, making us more resilient in the face of challenges.

Promoting Humility

A grateful heart recognizes that all we have is a gift from God. This recognition fosters humility, helping us to depend on God rather than our strength and resources.

Encouraging Obedience

Gratitude motivates us to live in obedience to God's commands. When we appreciate His blessings, we are more inclined to honor Him through our actions and choices.

Fostering Joy and Peace

Gratitude is closely linked to joy and peace. By focusing on God's goodness, we cultivate an inner sense of joy that transcends our circumstances and a peace that guards our hearts and minds (Philippians 4:7).

Building Community and Unity

Gratitude encourages us to build and maintain strong, positive relationships within the community of believers. A grateful heart contributes to a culture of mutual support and encouragement, enhancing the unity and effectiveness of the Church.

Inspiring Generosity

Recognizing God's blessings inspires us to give generously to others. Gratitude shifts our focus from receiving to giving, fostering a spirit of generosity that reflects God's character.

Deepening Worship

A grateful heart enhances our worship, making it more heartfelt and genuine. As we recognize and appreciate God's blessings, our worship becomes a true reflection of our love and thankfulness.

Overcoming Ingratitude: Lessons From The Israelites

The Israelites' journey offers valuable lessons on overcoming ingratitude. Their repeated failures to appreciate God's faithfulness highlight the importance of intentional practices to maintain a grateful heart.

One of the key lessons is the importance of remembering and recounting God's past faithfulness. The Israelites often forgot the miracles God had performed for them, leading to doubt and ingratitude. To avoid this, we must intentionally remember and celebrate God's work.

Regular worship helps to keep our hearts focused on God's goodness. By praising Him in both good times and bad, we reinforce our awareness of His constant presence and provision.

Understanding that trials are opportunities for spiritual growth can help us maintain gratitude even in difficult times. Recognizing that God is refining our faith through challenges enables us to see beyond our current struggles to their greater purpose.

Surrounding ourselves with a supportive community of believers encourages gratitude and discourages ingratitude. Sharing testimonies and supporting one another fosters a culture of thankfulness and mutual encouragement.

Contentment is a natural byproduct of a grateful heart. By learning to be content with what we have, we reduce the tendency to grumble and complain, focusing instead on God's blessings.

Practical Applications: Living A Life Of Gratitude

To fully embrace gratitude and its transformative power, it is essential to implement practical applications in our daily lives. Here are some strategies to help integrate gratitude into your lifestyle:

- Start with Prayer

Begin each day with a prayer of thanksgiving, acknowledging God's presence and blessings. This sets a positive tone for the day and cultivates a grateful mindset.

- Set Aside Time for Gratitude

Dedicate specific times in your day for reflecting on what you are thankful for. This could be during your morning routine, lunch break, or before bed.

- Share Your Blessings

Regularly share your blessings with others, whether through conversation, social media, or acts of service. Sharing gratitude reinforces your thankfulness and spreads positivity to those around you.

- Practice Forgiveness

Ungratefulness can sometimes stem from unresolved grievances. Practicing forgiveness frees your heart from bitterness, allowing gratitude to flourish.

- Focus on Solutions, Not Problems

When faced with challenges, consciously shift your focus from the problems to the solutions and the ways God is helping you overcome them. This positive outlook fosters gratitude even in adversity.

- Create Visual Reminders

Use visual aids such as gratitude boards, sticky notes, or inspirational quotes to remind yourself of God's blessings throughout the day.

- Engage in Regular Fasting

Fasting can heighten your spiritual awareness and appreciation for God's provision. It creates space for reflection and gratitude by removing distractions.

- Develop Gratitude Rituals

Incorporate gratitude into daily rituals, such as meals, family gatherings, or personal devotions. These rituals can reinforce a habit of thankfulness.

Testimonies Of Gratitude

Personal testimonies of gratitude can serve as powerful illustrations of its impact. Consider the story of a believer who, despite facing severe trials, maintained a spirit of thankfulness and experienced a profound transformation.

Sarah's Journey through Illness

Sarah was diagnosed with a serious illness that left her physically weak and emotionally drained. Instead of succumbing to despair, she chose to focus on the blessings in her life—her supportive family, her faith community, and the moments of joy she still experienced. By maintaining a gratitude journal, Sarah documented daily blessings, no matter how small. This practice shifted her perspective from what she had lost to what she still possessed, strengthening her faith and providing emotional resilience. Through her journey, Sarah became a beacon of hope and gratitude, inspiring others to find joy amid suffering.

Mark's Financial Struggles

Mark faced significant financial difficulties that threatened his ability to support his family. Instead of allowing stress and anxiety to take over, he chose to trust in God's provision. Mark began to express gratitude for the little he had and sought opportunities to help others despite his struggles. His attitude of thankfulness brought peace to his household and opened doors for unexpected blessings and support from his community. Mark's story illustrates how gratitude can transform adversity into a testimony of God's faithfulness.

The Role Of Gratitude In Enhancing Our Witness

A life marked by gratitude is a powerful testimony to the world of God's goodness. When others see us expressing thankfulness despite our circumstances, it reflects the transformative power of faith and can draw others to seek the source of our joy.

Authentic Testimony

Gratitude provides an authentic testimony of our relationship with God. It shows that our faith is not contingent on our circumstances but is rooted in a deep trust in God's character.

Overcoming Negativity

In a world often dominated by negativity and complaints, a grateful attitude stands out. It challenges the prevailing culture of discontent and invites others to experience the joy of gratitude.

Building Bridges

Gratitude fosters positive relationships and builds bridges of understanding and cooperation. It creates an environment where love and appreciation can flourish, enhancing our ability to connect with others on a meaningful level.

Reflecting God's Nature

Our gratitude reflects the nature of God, who is gracious, merciful, and loving. By expressing thankfulness, we mirror His attributes and glorify Him in our daily lives.

Embracing Gratitude In The Drama Of Life

To be an actor in God's drama, we must embrace gratitude as a central theme in our lives. Just as the Israelites' ingratitude led them into deeper troubles, our unthankfulness can hinder our spiritual journey and our ability to face life's high waves. However, by cultivating a heart of gratitude, we align ourselves with God's purposes and empower ourselves to overcome adversity with grace and strength.

Make gratitude a daily practice, integrating it into every aspect of your life. This consistent focus on thankfulness helps to reinforce a positive and resilient mindset.

Encourage and support one another in cultivating gratitude within your faith community. Shared expressions of thankfulness can strengthen the collective faith and provide mutual encouragement.

Translate gratitude into action by serving others, giving generously, and living out your faith in tangible ways. Acts of kindness and service are expressions of a grateful heart and demonstrate God's love for the world.

Recognize that cultivating gratitude is an ongoing process. Continuously seek to grow in thankfulness through spiritual disciplines, reflection, and intentional practice.

Embracing Gratitude Amid High Waves

Ungratefulness is a formidable adversary that can weaken our soul and obscure our perception of God's goodness. The Israelites' history of ingratitude serves as a powerful reminder of the consequences of forgetting God's faithfulness. However, by cultivating a heart of gratitude, we can counteract the poison of ungratefulness and navigate the high waves of life with confidence and resilience.

Gratitude transforms our perspective, strengthens our faith, and deepens our relationship with God. It empowers us to face challenges with a steadfast spirit, knowing that God is with us and working all things for our good. As we embrace gratitude, we become active participants in God's drama, shining His light in a world that desperately needs to see His goodness.

Let us commit to fostering gratitude in our hearts, remembering God's countless blessings, and expressing thankfulness in every circumstance. In doing so, we not only protect ourselves from the consequences of ungratefulness but also become vessels through which God's love and faithfulness are proclaimed to the world.

Key Takeaways

- **Recognize the Dangers of Ungratefulness:** Understand how ingratitude can weaken your faith, foster discontentment, and damage relationships.
- **Learn from Biblical Examples:** Reflect on the Israelites' history of ingratitude to appreciate the importance of maintaining a grateful heart.

- **Cultivate a Grateful Heart:** Implement spiritual disciplines such as daily reflection, gratitude journaling, and worship to develop and sustain gratitude.

- **Overcome Ingratitude with Practical Steps:** Utilize practical strategies like setting gratitude reminders, journaling daily blessings, and intentionally expressing thankfulness to God and others.

These actions help shift your focus from what's missing to what's already been provided, transforming your perspective and opening your heart to receive even more of God's goodness. Remember, gratitude is a powerful force that not only honors God but also fortifies your spirit, enabling you to stand strong amidst life's challenges.

CHAPTER
FIVE

Align yourself with
God's script, and the waves
that were meant to drown
you will carry you to
your destiny.

APOSTLE DR. DAVID PHILEMON

CHAPTER FIVE

ALIGNING WITH GOD'S SCRIPT

E very story has a script—a carefully crafted plan that guides the narrative from beginning to end. There is a divine script already written about your life and destiny. In the grand drama of life, God is the ultimate playwright, having written a script for each of us. This divine script is not just a series of events or a blueprint for living; it is a profound expression of God's will and purpose for our lives. Aligning with God's script means embracing His plan, trusting His timing, and following His lead, even when the path seems uncertain or the waves rise high.

In this chapter, we explore the concept of aligning with God's script, using the story of Joseph as a powerful illustration. We will delve into the significance of trusting God's plan, the challenges of staying aligned with His script, and the ultimate victory that comes from obedience and faithfulness.

The Story Of Joseph: A Model Of Alignment

The life of Joseph, as recorded in the book of Genesis, serves as a quintessential example of what it means to align with God's script. Joseph's journey was marked by a series of dramatic twists and turns—betrayal, slavery, false accusations, and imprisonment. Yet, through it all, Joseph remained steadfast in his faith and aligned with God's plan.

Joseph's Dreams: A Glimpse of the Script

Joseph's journey began with two prophetic dreams (Genesis 37:5-11), which hinted at his future greatness. In these dreams, Joseph saw his brothers bowing down to him, symbolizing his eventual rise to power. However, these dreams also set the stage for the trials he would face, as his brothers' jealousy led them to sell him into slavery.

5 One night Joseph had a dream, and when he told his brothers about it, they hated him more than ever.

6 "Listen to this dream," he said.

7 "We were out in the field, tying up bundles of grain. Suddenly my bundle stood up, and your bundles all gathered around and bowed low before mine!"

8 His brothers responded, "So you think you will be our king, do you? Do you actually think you will reign over us?" And they hated him all the more because of his dreams and the way he talked about them.

~ GENESIS 37:5-8 TLB

From the outset, Joseph's life was aligned with God's script, even though the fulfillment of the dreams seemed impossible. The key to Joseph's success was his unwavering faith in God's plan, even when the circumstances were dire.

Betrayal And Slavery: The Beginning Of The Journey

Joseph's descent into slavery was the first of many trials that tested his alignment with God's script. Sold by his brothers and taken to Egypt, Joseph found himself in a foreign land, stripped of his freedom and family. Yet, even in these harsh conditions, Joseph continued to trust in God.

3 Potiphar noticed this and realized that the Lord was with Joseph in a very special way.

4 So Joseph naturally became quite a favorite with him. Soon he was put in charge of the administration of Potiphar's household, and all of his business affairs.

5 At once the Lord began blessing Potiphar for Joseph'ssake.

~ GENESIS 39:3-5 TLB

Rather than succumbing to despair, Joseph worked diligently and faithfully in Potiphar's house, eventually rising to a position of authority (Genesis39:1-6). His integrity and commitment to excellence reflected alignment with God's script, demonstrating that even in the lowest points, God's plan was still at work.

False Accusation And Imprisonment: Testing Faith

Just as Joseph began to find stability in Potiphar's house, another wave of adversity struck. Potiphar's wife falsely accused Joseph of attempting to seduce her, leading to his imprisonment (Genesis 39:7-20). This turn of events could have easily led Joseph to question God's plan. However, Joseph remained faithful, trusting that even this unjust imprisonment was part of the divine script.

In prison, Joseph continued to exhibit the qualities of a man aligned with God's will. He earned the trust of the prison warden and was placed in charge of the other prisoners (Genesis39:21-23). This position eventually led to his encounter with Pharaoh's cupbearer and baker, which would later be pivotal in Joseph's rise to power.

Interpreting Dreams: A Step Toward Destiny

Joseph's gift of dream interpretation became a critical tool in his journey. While in prison, Joseph interpreted the dreams of Pharaoh's cupbearer and baker, accurately predicting their futures (Genesis 40:1-23). Two years later, this gift would bring him before Pharaoh, who was troubled by his dreams (Genesis 41:1-14).

Joseph's interpretation of Pharaoh's dreams—predicting seven years of abundance followed by seven years of famine—demonstrated not only his prophetic insight but also his unwavering alignment with God's script. His faithfulness in smaller tasks led to greater responsibilities, ultimately positioning him as second in command over all of Egypt (Genesis 41:39-41).

39 Turning to Joseph, Pharaoh said to him, "Since God has revealed the meaning of the dreams to you, you are the wisest man in the country!

40 I am hereby appointing you to be in charge of this entire project. What you say goes, throughout all the land of Egypt. I alone will outrank you."

~ GENESIS 41:39-41 TLB

RISING TO POWER: FULFILLMENT OF THE SCRIPT

Joseph's rise to power was the culmination of his alignment with God's script. As governor of Egypt, Joseph implemented a plan to store grain during the years of abundance, ensuring survival during the famine. This plan not only saved Egypt but also brought his brothers—the same ones who had betrayed him—down to Egypt in search of food (Genesis 42-45).

In one of the most poignant moments in the Bible, Joseph revealed his identity to his brothers and declared, "You intended to harm me, but God intended it for good to accomplish what is now being done, the saving of many lives" (Genesis 50:20).

"As far as I am concerned, God turned into good what you meant for evil, for he brought me to this high position I have today so that I could save the lives of many people."

~ GENESIS 50:20 TLB

This statement encapsulates the essence of aligning with God's script: no matter the trials or setbacks, God's plan is always for our good and His glory.

Challenges In Aligning With God's Script

Aligning with God's script is not without its challenges. Life's high waves—symbolic of trials, temptations, and uncertainties—can easily cause us to lose sight of God's plan. However, these challenges are integral to the process of spiritual growth and maturity.

The Temptation to Deviate

One of the greatest challenges in aligning with God's script is the temptation to deviate from it. When faced with difficult circumstances, we may be tempted to take matters into our own hands, pursuing our plans instead of waiting on God. Joseph faced this temptation numerous times, yet he chose to remain faithful to God's plan.

Deviating from God's script often leads to unnecessary pain and complications. Like Jonah, who tried to flee from God's calling and ended up in the belly of a great fish (Jonah 1:17), when we stray from the path God has set for us, we find ourselves in situations that could have been avoided had we trusted in His plan.

The Pain Of Patience

Another challenge in aligning with God's script is the pain of patience. God's timing is often different from our own, and waiting for His plan to unfold can be difficult. Joseph spent years in slavery and imprisonment before his dreams were fulfilled. This waiting period was not wasted time but a season of preparation.

Patience is a virtue that is cultivated through trials. As James 1:3-4 reminds us, *"The testing of your faith produces perseverance. Let perseverance finish its work so that you may be mature and complete, not lacking anything."* The high waves of life teach us patience, helping us to trust in God's timing rather than our own.

The Struggle With Doubt

Doubt is a natural human response to adversity. When the waves are high and the storm seems unrelenting, it is easy to doubt God's plan. Joseph, too, must have faced moments of doubt, yet he chose to hold on to his faith.

Doubt can be a dangerous obstacle, leading us to question God's goodness and His control over our lives. However, it is in these moments of doubt that we are called to reaffirm our trust in God. Like Peter, who walked on water until he began to doubt and start to sink (Matthew 14:29-30), we must keep our eyes fixed on Jesus, trusting that He will sustain us through the storm. A man who is doubtful misaligned and considered unstable in his ways and thus cannot receive anything from God.

7-8 and every decision you then make will be uncertain, as you turn first this way and then that. If you don't ask with faith, don't expect the Lord to give you any solid answer.

~ JAMES 1:7-8 TLB

The Victory Of AlignmenT

The story of Joseph demonstrates that aligning with God's script ultimately leads to victory. This victory is not always immediate or apparent, but it is assured. When we follow God's plan, even the most challenging circumstances can be used for good.

Divine Promotion

Joseph's journey from the pit to the palace illustrates the principle of divine promotion. When we align with God's script, He elevates us in His timing and according to His purpose. Joseph's promotion to governor of Egypt was not just a reward for his faithfulness; it was part of God's greater plan to save many lives.

God's promotion often comes after a season of testing and refinement. Like gold that is purified in the fire, our character is developed through trials, preparing us for the responsibilities that come with promotion.

Fulfillment of Purpose

Aligning with God's script leads to the fulfillment of our divine purpose. Joseph's purpose was not only to rise to power but to preserve a remnant of God's people during the famine. His entire journey, with all its ups and downs, was directed toward this ultimate purpose.

Each of us has a unique purpose that God has woven into His script for our lives. When we align with His plan, we step into that purpose, experiencing the joy and fulfillment that come from living in harmony with God's will.

The Impact on Others

Joseph's alignment with God's script did not only affect his life; it had a profound impact on others. His actions saved his family and countless others from starvation. Similarly, when we align with God's plan, our lives become a testimony to His goodness and faithfulness, impacting those around us.

Our obedience and faithfulness can inspire others to trust in God's plan for their own lives. Just as Joseph's brothers eventually recognized God's hand in their situation, those around us may come to see the power of God's script through our example.

Trusting The Divine Playwright

The high waves of life are inevitable, but they are not meant to drown us. When we align with God's script, we find that even the most challenging circumstances are part of His greater plan for our lives. Like Joseph, we can rise above the waves, trusting that God's plan is perfect and that He will bring us to victory.

Aligning with God's script requires faith, patience, and perseverance. It is a journey of trust, where we learn to let go of our plans and embrace the divine narrative that God has written for us. In doing so, we discover that the high waves, which once seemed daunting, are not meant to overwhelm us but to elevate us. They carry us to places we never imagined, revealing new depths of God's grace and power. As we surrender to His script, we find that every twist and turn, every challenge and triumph, is part of a greater story that leads to our ultimate destiny and fulfillment in Him.

CHAPTER
SIX

True power lies in synergy
—when aligned purposes
converge under
God's divine direction.

APOSTLE DR. DAVID PHILEMON

CHAPTER SIX

THE POWER OF SYNERGY

Synergy is a principle that goes beyond simple teamwork or collaboration. It is the phenomenon where the combined power of aligned purposes creates an effect greater than the sum of individual efforts. In the context of our spiritual journey, synergy is about aligning with God's purpose and partnering with others who share that vision, thus amplifying the impact of our collective efforts. When we understand and harness the power of synergy, we unlock a force that can propel us toward our divine destiny, overcoming obstacles and achieving what would be impossible alone.

Synergy In The Scriptures: A Divine Principle

The concept of synergy is deeply rooted in the Bible, where it is often illustrated through the power of unity and collective action. One of the most profound examples of synergy is found in the ministry of Jesus Christ. Jesus understood the power of synergy, and He deliberately surrounded Himself with disciples who shared His mission and vision.

13 Afterwards he went up into the hills and summoned certain ones he chose, inviting them to come and join him there; and they did.

14-15 Then he selected twelve of them to be his regular companions and to go out to preach and to cast out demons.

~ MARK 3:13-15TLB

This small group of twelve men, despite their flaws and differences, became a powerful force for the Kingdom of God because they were united in purpose and aligned with God's will.

The early Church also exemplified the power of synergy. In Acts 2, we see the believers coming together with one heart and mind, sharing everything they had and supporting one another. This unity and alignment with God's purpose resulted in extraordinary growth and impact, as *"the Lord added to their number daily those who were being saved"* (Acts 2:47). The collective power of the early church, fueled by the Holy Spirit, changed the course of history and laid the foundation for Christianity as we know it today.

The Power Of Aligned Purposes

At the heart of synergy is the alignment of purposes. When individuals align their goals and actions with God's purpose, their combined efforts are multiplied. This principle is evident in various aspects of life, including business, sports, and relationships, but it is especially powerful in the spiritual realm.

Partnership In Creation

The concept of partnership is evident from the very beginning of creation. In Genesis 1, we see the Trinity—Father, Son, and Holy Spirit—working in perfect harmony to create the universe. Each Person of the Trinity played a distinct role, yet their efforts were perfectly aligned, resulting in the creation of the world in all its complexity and beauty. This divine synergy set the pattern for all creation, showing us that when we align with God's purpose, we tap into a power that can bring forth life, order, and beauty from chaos.

Jesus And His Disciples: A Model Of Synergy

Jesus' relationship with His disciples is a powerful example of the impact of partnership. When Jesus called His disciples, He was not just assembling a group of followers; He was creating a team that would carry forward His mission after His departure. Each disciple brought unique gifts, talents, and perspectives, but what made them effective was their shared commitment to Jesus' mission. By aligning themselves with Jesus and each other, the disciples were able to accomplish far more than they could have individually.

This synergy was most evident after the resurrection, when the disciples, empowered by the Holy Spirit, began to spread the Gospel. Their united efforts, despite intense persecution, resulted in the rapid expansion of the Church and the transformation of countless lives. The power of synergy, underpinned by a shared vision and divine empowerment, enabled them to overcome obstacles and fulfill the Great Commission.

The Early Church: The Power Of Unity

The early Church provides another striking example of synergy. The believers were of *"one heart and one mind"* (Acts 4:32), and this unity allowed them to pool their resources, support one another, and spread the Gospel with unprecedented effectiveness.

"All the believers were of one heart and mind, and no one felt that what he owned was his own; everyone was sharing."

~ ACTS 4:32 TLB

Their alignment with God's purpose and with each other created a powerful partnership that shook the foundations of society and led to the explosive growth of the Christian faith.

This synergy was not just about numbers; it was about the

transformative power of a community that was fully aligned with God's will. The early Christians understood that they were part of something bigger than themselves, and this understanding fueled their commitment to each other and the mission. Their collective impact was far greater than what any one of them could have achieved alone, demonstrating the power of synergy in the body of Christ.

The Danger Of Misalignment: Spiritual Glaucoma

While synergy is a powerful force for good, it can also be hindered or even reversed by misalignment. In the spiritual context, misalignment occurs when individuals or groups are not in tune with God's purpose or when they partner with those who are spiritually blind. This condition, which can be likened to spiritual glaucoma, clouds vision and leads to impaired judgment and decision-making.

Spiritual Glaucoma: A Hindrance to Synergy

Spiritual glaucoma is a condition where individuals are unable to see the purpose and plan of God. Various factors, including pride, unbelief, and a lack of spiritual discernment can cause this blindness. When we align ourselves with those who suffer from spiritual glaucoma, we risk being led astray and missing out on the fullness of God's plan for our lives.

The Bible warns against such misalignment. In 2 Corinthians 6:14, Paul advises believers not to be "yoked together with unbelievers," as their differing purposes and values can lead to conflict and compromise.

"Don't be teamed with those who do not love the Lord, for what do the people of God have in common with the people of sin? How can light live with darkness?"

~ 2 CORINTHIANS 6:14 TLB

This principle applies not only to personal relationships but also to partnerships and alliances in ministry and other areas of life. Aligning with those who do not share a clear vision of God's purpose can hinder our progress and dilute the power of synergy.

The Consequences Of Misalignment

Misalignment can have serious consequences, both for individuals and for the broader body of Christ. When we are not aligned with God's purpose, we lose our effectiveness and our ability to impact the world for His Kingdom. Instead of experiencing the multiplied power of synergy, we find ourselves struggling, frustrated, and often defeated.

One of the most tragic examples of misalignment in the Bible is the story of King Saul. Saul started his reign with great promise, but he gradually drifted away from God's purpose. His failure to fully obey God's commands led to his downfall and the loss of his kingdom. Saul's misalignment not only affected him personally but also had a ripple effect on the entire nation of Israel, leading to a period of turmoil and instability.

In contrast, those who align themselves with God's purpose and with others who share that vision experience the full power of synergy. Their efforts are blessed, their impact is multiplied, and they fulfill the destiny that God has prepared for them.

Aligning With God's Purpose: A Call To Discernment

To harness the power of synergy, we must first ensure that we are aligned with God's purpose. This requires a deep level of spiritual discernment and a willingness to submit our plans and desires to God's will. It also means being selective about who we align with, ensuring that our ministry, business, and life partners share a clear vision of God's purpose.

Seeking God's Vision

The first step in aligning with God's purpose is seeking His vision for our lives. This involves spending time in prayer, studying the

Scriptures, and being attentive to the leading of the Holy Spirit. God's vision may not always be immediately apparent, but as we seek Him sincerely, He will reveal His plans to us.

Jesus often withdrew to solitary places to pray and seek the Father's will (Luke 5:16). This practice of seeking God's direction was a key factor in His ability to stay aligned with the Father's purpose, even in the face of intense opposition. Like Jesus, we must prioritize our relationship with God and seek His vision above all else.

Choosing the Right Partners

Once we are clear on God's purpose for our lives, the next step is to choose partners who share that vision. In the body of Christ, this means aligning ourselves with fellow believers who are committed to following God's script. It also means avoiding alliances with those who are spiritually blind or whose values and goals are not aligned with God's Kingdom.

The story of Jehoshaphat and Ahab in 2 Chronicles

18 is a cautionary tale about the dangers of aligning with the wrong partners. Jehoshaphat, a godly king, allied with Ahab, an ungodly ruler, and nearly lost his life. This alliance, based on political expediency rather than spiritual alignment, led to disastrous consequences. We must be discerning in our partnerships, ensuring that those we align with walk in the light of God's purpose.

Cultivating a Spirit of Unity

Collaboration is only possible when there is unity. In the body of Christ, unity is not just about agreeing on everything but about being united in purpose and mission. Paul exhorts the believers in Ephesians 4:3 to *"make every effort to keep the unity of the Spirit through the bond of peace.* "This unity is essential for the power of collaboration to be fully realized.

"Try always to be led along together by the Holy Spirit and so be at peace with one another."

~ EPHESIANS 4:3 TLB

Cultivating a spirit of unity requires humility, patience, and a willingness to put the needs of others above our own. It also involves being open to different perspectives and recognizing the value of diverse gifts and talents within the body of Christ. When we are united in purpose, the power of synergy is unleashed, and we can achieve far more together than we ever could alone.

The Unstoppable Force Of Synergy

When we align with God's purpose and join forces with others who share that vision, we become an unstoppable force for the Kingdom of God. The power of synergy enables us to overcome obstacles, break through barriers, and accomplish the impossible. It is a force that multiplies our efforts, amplifies our impact, and propels us toward our destiny.

Unity in Ministry

In ministry, the power of unity is essential for success. No one can fulfill God's mission alone; we need each other. The Apostle Paul understood this well, often working in partnership with others to plant churches, spread the Gospel, and disciple believers. In 1 Corinthians 3:6-9, Paul explains that while he planted the seed and Apollos watered it, it was God who made it grow.

6   My work was to plant the seed in your hearts, and Apollos' work was to water it, but it was God, not we, who made the garden grow in your hearts.

7   The person who does the planting or watering isn't very important, but God is important because he is the one who makes things grow.

8 Apollos and I are working as a team with the same aim, though

each of us will be rewarded for his hard work.

9 We are only God's coworkers. You are God's garden, not ours; you are God's building.

~ 1 CORINTHIANS 3:6-9 TLB

This is a perfect example of partnership in action—each person playing their part, but the result being far greater than the sum of their efforts.

Unity in the Body of Christ

The body of Christ is designed to function as a synergistic organism, with each member contributing their unique gifts and talents to the whole. Paul uses the analogy of the human body in 1 Corinthians 12 to illustrate this principle. Just as the body is made up of many parts, each with a different function, so the Church is made up of diverse individuals, each with a unique role to play. When each member is aligned with God's purpose and functioning in their God-given role, the body of Christ operates with maximum effectiveness, and the power of synergy is fully realized.

Unity in the World

The power of synergy is not limited to the Church; it can also have a profound impact on the world. When believers align with God's purpose and work together, they become a powerful force for change in society. Whether it's feeding the hungry, caring for the sick, or fighting for justice, the combined efforts of God's people can bring about transformation on a global scale.

The history of the Church is filled with exam ples of unity at work in the world. From the abolition of slavery to the civil rights movement, Christians united in purpose have played a key role in some of the most significant social changes in history. This is the power of unity—when God's people come together with a shared vision, there is no limit to what they can accomplish.

Embracing The Power Of Unity

The power of synergy is a divine gift that God has given to His people. When we align with God's purpose and join forces with others who share that vision, we tap into a supernatural force that can change the world. However, to fully experience the power of synergy, we must be intentional about aligning ourselves with God's script and choosing the right partners. We must also cultivate a spirit of unity within the body of Christ, recognizing that we are stronger together than we are apart.

As we embrace the power of unity, we will see God do amazing things in and through us. The high waves of life may come, but with the power of synergy, we will not only survive—we will thrive. We will accomplish more than we ever dreamed possible, and in the process, we will bring glory to God and advance His Kingdom on earth. The power of synergy is available to all who are willing to align with God's purpose and join forces with others who share that vision. Let us embrace it fully and watch as God uses us to do the impossible.

March forward with divine orders, for obedience paves the path to victory.

APOSTLE DR. DAVID PHILEMON

CHAPTER SEVEN

MARCHING ORDERS FOR DEFEATING THE HIGH WAVES

As believers, we are called to rise to a higher level of responsibility and purpose in our walk with God—A Higher Calling. The journey of faith is not static; it requires growth, maturity, and an unwavering commitment to God's plan. In this chapter, we will explore nine critical steps —marching orders—that will help you stay aligned with God's purpose and navigate the high waves of life with confidence and strength. These steps are not just guidelines but essential directives for anyone seeking to fulfill their divine calling.

Align Yourself with God's Script

The first and most crucial marching order is to align yourself with God's script. God's plan for your life is perfect, and it is only by following His script that you can experience true victory. This alignment requires surrendering your plans, desires, and ambitions to God, trusting that His ways are higher and better than yours.

In the story of Joseph, we see the power of aligning with God's script. Despite the betrayals, false accusations, and imprisonment he faced, Joseph remained faithful to God's plan. In the end, his alignment with God's purpose led him to a position of power and influence, allowing him to save many lives.

"As far as I am concerned, God turned into good what you meant for evil, for he brought me to this high position I have today so that I could save the lives of many people."

~ GENESIS 50:20 TLB

Like Joseph, you must trust that God's script for your life will lead to a victorious outcome, even when the path seems difficult or unclear.

Aligning with God's script also means being sensitive to His leading and being willing to make adjustments when necessary. There may be times when God redirects your path or calls you to step out in faith in ways that challenge your comfort zone. In these moments, it is essential to stay connected to God through prayer, worship, and the study of His Word, ensuring that you are always in tune with His voice.

Intercede for Others

Intercession is a powerful tool in the believer's arsenal. When you intercede for others, you are standing in the gap, asking God to intervene in their lives in miraculous ways. The Bible is full of examples of intercession, where individuals prayed for divine interceptions, interjections, and ejections of contradictions in the lives of others.

One of the most notable examples of intercession is found in Psalm 106:23, where Moses interceded for the Israelites after they had sinned by creating the golden calf. God was ready to destroy the entire nation, but Moses stepped in and pleaded with God to spare them. His intercession led to God's mercy and the preservation of the people.

Intercession is not just about praying for others; it is about partnering with God to bring about His will on earth. When you intercede, you are engaging in spiritual warfare, battling against the forces of darkness that seek to hinder God's plans. This requires persistence, faith, and a deep love for those you are praying for. As you intercede, you are participating in God's redemptive work, helping to bring about His kingdom's purposes in the lives of others.

Take Action

Faith without works is dead (James 2:26).

"Just as the body is dead when there is no spirit in it, so faith is dead if it is not the kind that results in good deeds."

~ JAMES 2:26 TLB

Believing in God's promises is important, but it is not enough to simply have faith—you must also take action. This marching order calls you to move beyond passive belief and actively engage in the work God has called you to do.

Taking action requires courage and a willingness to step out in faith, even when the outcome is uncertain. It means putting your faith into practice by obeying God's instructions, serving others, and pursuing the vision He has placed in your heart. Whether it is starting a new ministry, helping those in need, or sharing the Gospel with someone who has never heard it, taking action is a vital part of living out your faith.

Consider the example of the Israelites at the Red Sea. When they were trapped between the sea and the Egyptian army, God instructed Moses to *"raise your staff and stretch out your hand over the sea to divide the water so that the Israelites can go through the sea on dry ground"* (Exodus 14:16). Moses had to take action—he had to raise his staff and stretch out his hand—before the miracle could occur. Likewise, you must be willing to take steps of faith, trusting that God will meet you in your obedience and bring about

His miraculous intervention.

Develop Spiritual Discernment

In today's world, where countless voices and influences are vying for our attention, developing spiritual discernment is more important than ever. Discernment is the ability to distinguish between what is from God and what is not. It is the skill of recognizing the spiritual forces at work behind situations, people, and decisions.

The Apostle Paul demonstrated spiritual discernment when he encountered a slave girl in Philippi who had a spirit of divination (Acts 16:17-18).

17   She followed along behind us shouting, "These men are servants of God, and they have come to tell you how to have your sins forgiven."

18   This went on day after day until Paul, in great distress, turned and spoke to the demon within her. "I command you in the name of Jesus Christ to come out of her," he said. And instantly it left her.

~ ACTS 16:17-18 TLB

Although the girl was saying things that seemed positive, Paul discerned that the spirit behind her words was not from God. He cast out the spirit, freeing the girl and demonstrating the power of spiritual discernment.

To develop spiritual discernment, you must cultivate a deep relationship with God through prayer, meditation on His Word, and a reliance on the Holy Spirit. The Holy Spirit is your guide and teacher, leading you into all truth and helping you to discern the spiritual landscape.

Additionally, it is important to surround yourself with mature believers who can offer wise counsel and help you navigate complex situations.

Spiritual discernment is not just about avoiding deception; it is also about making wise decisions that align with God's will. It enables you to see beyond the surface and understand the deeper spiritual realities at play. As you grow in discernment, you will be better equipped to make decisions that honor God and advance His kingdom.

Stay Firm and Steadfast

The journey of faith is not always easy. There will be times of trial, testing, and opposition. In these moments, it is essential to stay firm and steadfast, holding on to your faith and God's promises. Stability and reliability are key qualities of a mature believer—someone God and others can count on, no matter the circumstances.

Staying firm and steadfast requires a deep-rooted faith that is not easily shaken by external challenges. It means remaining committed to God's Word, even when it contradicts popular opinion or cultural trends. It also means persevering in prayer, worship, and service, even when you feel discouraged or weary.

The Apostle Paul, writing to the Corinthians, encouraged them to *"stand firm in the faith; be courageous; be strong"* (1 Corinthians 16:13). This exhortation is a reminder that our strength, and stability come from our faith in God. As you stay firm and steadfast, you will find that God strengthens you, giving you the endurance to overcome challenges and continue on the path He has set.

Guard Your Heart

The condition of your heart is critical to your spiritual health and effectiveness. The Bible tells us to "above all else, guard your heart, for everything you do flows from it" (Proverbs 4:23).

"So above all, guard the affections of your heart, for they affect all that you are. Pay attention to the welfare of your innermost being, for from there flows the wellspring of life."

~ PROVERBS 4:23 TPT

Your heart is the wellspring of your thoughts, emotions, and actions, and if it becomes polluted with bitterness, anger, or unforgiveness, it can hinder your relationship with God and your ability to fulfill His purpose.

One of the greatest threats to your heart is bitterness. Bitterness can take root when you hold on to past hurts, disappointments, or offenses. It can grow and fester, eventually destabilizing your faith and leading you away from God. Psalm 106:33 reminds us of how bitterness affected Moses, causing him to speak rashly and ultimately leading to his exclusion from the Promised Land.

To guard your heart, you must be intentional about cultivating gratitude, forgiveness, and love. Gratitude shifts your focus from what is wrong to what is right, helping you to see God's goodness in every situation. Forgiveness frees you from the bondage of bitterness and allows you to move forward in your walk with God. Love, the greatest commandment, keeps your heart aligned with God's character and purposes.

Remain Focused

Distraction is one of the enemy's most effective tools to derail believers from their divine purpose. Amid the high waves and the chaos of life, it is easy to lose focus on what truly matters—your relationship with Jesus and the mission He has given you. Remaining focused requires discipline, determination, and a clear understanding of your priorities.

In Matthew 14:31, we see the story of Peter walking on water toward Jesus. As long as Peter kept his eyes on Jesus, he was able to do the impossible. But when he became distracted by the wind and the waves, he began to sink. This story is a powerful reminder of the importance of staying focused on Jesus, no matter the circumstances.

To remain focused, you must eliminate distractions that pull you away from God's purpose. This may involve setting boundaries, simplifying your life, and making intentional choices to prioritize your time with God. It also means keeping your eyes on the eternal, rather than getting caught up in the temporary concerns of this world. As you remain focused on Jesus, He will guide you through the storms and lead you safely to your destination.

Verify the Spirit behind the Information

Not everything that glitters is gold. In a world filled with information, it is essential to verify the spirit behind what you hear, see, and experience. The Apostle John warns us to *"test the spirits to see whether they are from God"*(1 John 4:1).

"Delightfully loved friends, don't trust every spirit, but carefully examine what they say to determine if they are of God, because many false prophets have mingled into the world."

~ 1 JOHN 4:1 TPT

This marching order calls you to exercise discernment and caution, ensuring that the information you receive aligns with God's truth.

The importance of verifying the spirit behind the information cannot be overstated. Deception is rampant, and the enemy often disguises himself as an angel of light (2 Corinthians 11:14).

"That doesn't surprise us, for even Satan transforms himself to appear as an angel of light!"

~ 2 CORINTHIANS 11:14 TPT

To protect yourself from deception, you must measure everything against the Word of God. The Bible is your ultimate standard for truth and anything that contradicts it should be rejected.

In addition to testing the spirits, it is important to seek the guidance of the Holy Spirit in all things. The Holy Spirit will lead you into all truth and help you discern what is from God and what is not. By verifying the spirit behind the information, you can avoid falling into traps and stay on the path that God has set for you.

Pursue Spiritual Maturity

The final marching order is to pursue spiritual maturity. God does not want you to remain a spiritual infant, content with milk when He has meat to offer (Hebrews 5:12-14).

"For you should already be professors instructing others by now; but instead, you need to be taught from the beginning the basics of God's prophetic oracles! You're like children still needing milk and not yet ready to digest solid food."

~ HEBREWS5:12-14 TPT

Spiritual maturity involves growing your knowledge of God, deepening your relationship with Him, and becoming more like Christ in your character and actions.

Pursuing spiritual maturity requires intentional effort and commitment. It involves studying the Word of God, engaging in regular prayer and worship, and participating in the life of the Church. It also means being open to correction, willing to learn from others, and desiring to grow in your faith.

As you pursue spiritual maturity, you will find that your capacity to fulfill God's purpose increases. You will be better equipped to handle the challenges and responsibilities that come with your calling. Spiritual maturity also leads to greater intimacy with God, as you learn to hear His voice more clearly and follow His leading more closely.

Marching Forward With Confidence

These nine marching orders are not just a list of suggestions—they are critical steps for anyone who wants to stay on track in their walk with God. As you align yourself with God's script, intercede for others, take action, develop spiritual discernment, stay firm and steadfast, guard your heart, remain focused, verify the Spirit behind the information, and pursue spiritual maturity, you will be equipped to navigate the high waves of life with confidence.

God is calling you to step into a higher place of responsibility and purpose. The journey may not always be easy, but with these marching orders, you will have the tools you need to stay on course and fulfill your divine calling. As you march forward with faith and determination, you can be assured that God is with you every step of the way, guiding you, strengthening you, and leading you to victory.

CHAPTER EIGHT

Stability is the anchor that holds you firm when life's waves threaten to topple you.

APOSTLE DR. DAVID PHILEMON

CHAPTER EIGHT

THE GIFT OF STABILITY

Stability is more than just a desirable trait; it is a divine gift that allows us to remain unshaken amid life's most tumultuous storms. In a world where chaos and uncertainty seem to reign, stability becomes not only a refuge but also a powerful force that enables us to fulfill our God-given purpose. The importance of this gift cannot be overstated, especially for believers who are called to be the light and salt in a world that desperately needs both.

The Nature Of Stability

Stability, as a concept, is often misunderstood. It is not about rigidity or being resistant to change; rather, it is about having a firm foundation that allows us to adapt without being uprooted. It is the ability to remain grounded and steadfast, no matter what external forces may come our way. In the spiritual realm, stability is rooted in our relationship with God and our understanding of His Word. It is the anchor that holds us steady when the high waves of life threaten to overwhelm us.

In Matthew 7:24-27, Jesus gives us a vivid illustration of what it means to have this kind of stability. He compares two builders: one wise and the other foolish. The wise builder constructs his house on a rock, ensuring that it has a solid foundation. The foolish builder, on the other hand, builds his house on sand, which offers no stability. When the storms come—and they always do—

the house on the rock stands firm, while the house on the sand collapses. This parable underscores the importance of having our lives built on the solid rock of God's Word. Only then can we withstand the storms that life inevitably brings.

The Threat Of Destabilization

The enemy is acutely aware of the power of stability, which is why one of his primary strategies is to destabilize believers. He knows that a stable Christian is a formidable force in the kingdom of God. Therefore, he works tirelessly to sow seeds of doubt, fear, and confusion, hoping to uproot us from our firm foundation.

Distractions are one of the enemy's most effective tools to destabilize us. These distractions can come in many forms: financial pressures, relationship issues, health challenges, or even the allure of worldly success. While these things are not inherently evil, they become problematic when they divert our focus from God and His purpose for our lives. When we allow distractions to take root in our hearts, we lose our stability. Our once-solid foundation starts to feel shaky; before we know it, we are vulnerable to the enemy's attacks.

Another tactic the enemy uses is isolation. By separating us from the community of believers, he weakens our defenses. The Bible tells us that we are like sheep, and sheep are safest when they are together under the watchful eye of the shepherd. When a sheep wanders off on its own, it becomes an easy predator target. Similarly, when we isolate ourselves from the body of Christ, we become easy prey for the enemy. We lose the strength from corporate prayer, worship, and fellowship, and our stability begins to erode.

Building On The Rock

To combat the threats, we must intentionally build our lives on the rock of God's Word. This requires more than just a superficial acquaintance with the Scriptures; it demands a deep, personal relationship with the Word, which is Jesus Christ Himself. We must immerse ourselves in the Bible, allowing its truths to permeate every aspect of our lives. The more we know and apply God's Word, the more stable we become.

Prayer is another critical component of building stability. Through prayer, we communicate with God, align ourselves with His will, and receive the strength we need to stand firm. Prayer keeps us connected to our source of stability, ensuring that the changing tides of life do not sway us. When we make prayer a priority, we build a strong, unbreakable connection with God that fortifies us against the enemy's schemes.

Worship also plays a crucial role in maintaining stability. When we worship, we shift our focus from our problems to the greatness of God. Worship reminds us of who God is and what He has done, reinforcing our faith and anchoring us in His promises. In the act of worship, we find our true center, grounding ourselves in the unchanging character of God.

The Fruits Of Stability

Stability is not an end in itself; it produces fruit in our lives that glorifies God and blesses others. One of the primary fruits of stability is **peace.** When we are stable, we experience a deep, abiding peace that transcends our circumstances. This peace is not dependent on external conditions but is rooted in our confidence in God's sovereignty. As Paul writes in Philippians 4:7, it is the "peace of God, which transcends all understanding," that guards our hearts and minds in Christ Jesus. This kind of peace is a powerful witness to a world that is often characterized by anxiety and turmoil.

Another fruit of stability is **resilience.** A stable person can bounce back from setbacks and challenges without being defeated. Life's storms may knock them down, but they are never out for the count. This resilience is not a result of personal strength but is a reflection of the strength that comes from being firmly rooted in

God. As Isaiah 40:31 reminds us, "Those who hope in the Lord will renew their strength. They will soar on wings like eagles; they will run and not grow weary; they will walk and not be faint."

Stability also leads to **consistency in** our walk with God. A stable believer is not swayed by every wind of doctrine or tossed about by the waves of popular opinion. They are steadfast in their faith, consistent in their spiritual disciplines, and unwavering in their commitment to God's truth. This consistency is a hallmark of spiritual maturity and is essential for effective ministry and witness.

Stability In Community

While individual stability is crucial, it is also important to recognize the role of the community in fostering stability. As the body of Christ, the church is meant to be a stable, supportive environment where believers can grow and thrive. In a healthy church community, members are encouraged, edified, and held accountable. This mutual support helps to reinforce stability, both individually and corporately.

In Ephesians 4:14-16, Paul emphasizes the importance of unity and maturity within the body of Christ. He writes, *"Then we will no longer be infants, tossed back and forth by the waves, and blown here and there by every wind of teaching... Instead, speaking the truth in love, we will grow to become in every respect the mature body of him who is the head, that is, Christ."*

Stability in the church comes from a collective commitment to truth, love, and maturity. When the body of Christ is stable, it becomes a powerful force for good in the world, able to withstand external pressures and fulfill its mission.

CHAPTER
NINE

The high waves of life are
designed to elevate you,
not devastate you.

APOSTLE DR. DAVID PHILEMON

CHAPTER NINE

THE HIGH WAVES

Life is full of challenges, trials, and unpredictable circumstances—what we can call the "high waves" of life. Though intimidating and often overwhelming, these waves are not meant to destroy us. Instead, they serve as a powerful means of strengthening our faith, revealing the true condition of our hearts, and drawing us closer to God.

The Purpose Of The High Waves

The high waves are not random occurrences but divinely orchestrated moments that test our faith and character. They are allowed by God for a purpose—often to expose the areas in our lives where we rely too much on our strength, intellect, or resources. These waves challenge us to shift our reliance from ourselves to God, who is our ultimate source of strength and stability.

Consider Peter's experience when he walked on water towards Jesus. As long as Peter kept his eyes on Jesus, he defied the natural laws of gravity and walked on the water's surface. However, the moment Peter shifted his focus to the wind and the waves, he began to sink. This story from Matthew 14:30 illustrates a fundamental truth: the high waves of life are not the real danger; the real danger lies in losing our focus on Jesus.

The Heart Revealed By The High Waves

High waves have a way of revealing what is hidden in the depths of our hearts. When everything is smooth sailing, it is easy to maintain an appearance of faith and strength. However, when the waves rise and the storms hit, our true beliefs, fears, and weaknesses are exposed. It is in these moments of trial that we discover whether our faith is superficial or deeply rooted in God's promises. The storms of life serve as a mirror, reflecting the condition of our hearts. Do we respond with panic and fear, or do we hold fast to our trust in God? Are we quick to blame God for our circumstances, or do we seek His guidance and strength? The high waves force us to confront these questions and grow in our spiritual maturity.

Drawing Closer To God Amid The Storm

The high waves are an invitation to draw closer to God. It is in the midst of the storm that we are reminded of our need for a Savior who can calm the seas. The waves may be high, but God is higher. He stands above the storm, sovereign and in control, ready to guide us through the turbulent waters.

When Peter began to sink, he cried out, "Lord, save me!" - "Sozo me." Immediately, Jesus reached out His hand and caught him. This moment of desperation became a powerful encounter with the Lord. Similarly, the high waves in our lives are opportunities to cry out to God, to reach for His hand, and to experience His saving power in a personal and profound way.

The Strength That Comes From Enduring The High Waves

Every wave that we face and overcome adds to our spiritual strength. The Apostle Paul, who faced numerous trials and hardships, wrote in Romans 5:3-4, "We also glory in our sufferings because we know that suffering produces perseverance; perseverance, character; and character, hope." The high waves, though challenging, are what shape us into resilient, hope-filled believers who can withstand the storms of life.

When we endure these trials, we develop a deeper faith that is not easily shaken. Our spiritual muscles are strengthened, and we become more equipped to handle future challenges. The high waves serve as training grounds, preparing us for greater responsibilities and victories in our walk with God.

Trusting God's Script In The High Waves

One of the most significant lessons the high waves teach us is to trust in God's script for our lives. Often, we have our ideas and plans about how life should unfold, but the waves disrupt these plans, reminding us that we are not in control. God, the ultimate Author, has written a script for our lives that is far better than anything we could imagine.

When we try to control every aspect of our lives, the high waves can feel overwhelming. However, when we surrender to God's will and trust His script, we find peace amid chaos. We learn to see the waves not as obstacles but as part of the journey that God has designed for our growth and ultimate good.

The Waves That Carry Us To New Heights

In God's hands, the very waves that threaten to drown us can become the means of our elevation. Just as the stormy sea carried Peter towards Jesus, the high waves in our lives can propel us to new heights of faith, maturity, and understanding. What the enemy intends for harm,

God can use it for our good.

The story of Joseph in the Old Testament is a powerful example of this principle. Joseph faced many high waves—betrayal, slavery, false accusations, and imprisonment. Yet, through it all, he remained faithful to God. In the end, the waves that sought to destroy him were the very waves that carried him to a position of power and influence, where he was able to save many lives (Genesis 50:20).

Similarly, when we align our lives with God's script, we discover that the high waves are not setbacks but setups for a greater purpose. The trials we endure become testimonies of God's faithfulness and power.

Embracing The High Waves

To embrace the high waves is to embrace the full experience of walking with God. It means accepting that life will have its challenges, but these challenges are not without purpose. They are opportunities to deepen our faith, grow in our relationship with God, and become the people He has called us to be.

Rather than fearing the high waves, we should welcome them as a necessary part of our spiritual journey. With our eyes fixed on Jesus, the waves lose their power to intimidate. We can walk on water, not because the waves have ceased, but because our focus is on the One who controls the waves.

The High Waves Of Life Are Not To Be Feared But Embraced.

They are tools in God's hands, used to refine us, strengthen us, and draw us closer to Him. As we navigate these waves with faith and trust in God's script, we will find that they do not have the power to destroy us. Instead, they will carry us to new heights, where we can experience the fullness of God's grace and the fulfillment of His purpose in our lives.

CHAPTER
TEN

In the quiet of low waves,
listen closely—God often
whispers His greatest
truths in the calm.

APOSTLE DR. DAVID PHILEMON

CHAPTER TEN

THE LOW WAVES
OF LIFE

When we think of waves, our minds often go to the towering, crashing swells that threaten to engulf us. These are the high waves of life, filled with drama, challenge, and the potential for great growth and victory. But life also has its low waves—those subtle, almost unnoticed forces that can erode our foundation if we're not careful. These low waves represent the quiet struggles, the everyday trials, and the persistent, nagging difficulties that slowly wear us down over time.

Understanding The Low Waves

Low waves are not the dramatic, life-altering events that grab our attention and demand immediate action. Instead, they are the small, seemingly insignificant issues that persist over time. These could be ongoing stress at work, unresolved conflicts in relationships, chronic health issues, or even the whisper of doubt and fear that erodes our confidence in God's promises.

In the same way that low-frequency sound waves, or infrasound, are often undetected by the human ear yet have the power to cause discomfort and even physical harm, the low waves of life operate subtly, often unnoticed until their cumulative effect becomes overwhelming. Infrasound, which can be generated by natural phenomena like earthquakes or man-made sources like machinery, can disturb and unsettle without being directly perceived. This phenomenon mirrors how the low waves of life can disturb our peace and stability if we are not vigilant.

The Persistent Erosion Of Low Waves

Consider the slow but steady erosion of the shoreline by gentle waves. Over time, even the smallest waves can wear away rocks, cliffs, and beaches, reshaping the landscape. Similarly, the low waves in our lives can slowly erode our spiritual, emotional, and physical well-being if we do not recognize and address them.

A biblical example of the low waves at work can be found in the story of the Israelites during their journey in the wilderness. While they faced dramatic high waves, like the parting of the Red Sea and the battle with the Amalekites, they also experienced the low waves of daily life in the desert. The persistent discomfort of wandering, the scarcity of food and water, and the constant waiting for God's promises to be fulfilled led to grumbling, doubt, and a gradual erosion of their faith and trust in God. Despite witnessing miraculous signs and wonders, their faith was slowly worn down by the everyday hardships they faced, leading to rebellion and a longer journey than God had intended (Numbers 14:22-23).

The Danger Of Ignoring The Low Waves

One of the greatest dangers of the low waves is that they are easy to ignore. Because they do not present an immediate, dramatic threat, we might dismiss them as unimportant or believe we can handle them on our own. However, this complacency can lead to a slow drift away from God's presence and purpose.

In Mark 4:19, Jesus warns about the subtle dangers of the low waves when He speaks of the "cares of this world, the deceitfulness of riches, and the desires for other things" that can choke the Word of God in our lives, making it unfruitful. These low waves are not overt sins but rather the everyday distractions and concerns that quietly pull us away from our focus on God. If left unchecked, they can lead to spiritual stagnation, preventing us from growing and bearing fruit in our Christian walk.

Real-Life Illustration: The Infrasound Of Life

Just as infrasound can cause unease and even harm without being consciously heard, the low waves of life can affect us without our full awareness. Imagine a person working in a noisy factory where infrasound is present. Over time, they might begin to feel irritable, anxious, or physically unwell without understanding the source of their discomfort. Similarly, the low waves of life—ongoing stress, unresolved issues, and unmet needs—can cause us to feel spiritually, emotionally, and physically drained without a clear understanding of why.

Take, for example, the life of King Saul in the Bible. His reign was marked by high waves, such as battles and direct encounters with prophets, but it was the low waves—the persistent jealousy of David, the fear of losing his kingdom, and the unresolved issues of disobedience to God—that slowly eroded his mental stability and spiritual health. These low waves were not as dramatic as the high waves, but they were equally destructive, leading to Saul's eventual downfall (1 Samuel 16:14-23, 18:6-12).

In our own lives, the low waves can manifest as chronic stress at work, ongoing conflicts in relationships, or a persistent sense of dissatisfaction or unfulfillment. These issues may not seem urgent, but their cumulative effect can be just as damaging as any major crisis if they are not addressed.

Counteracting The Low Waves

So, how do we deal with the low waves? The first step is awareness. Just as we need special equipment to detect infrasound, we need spiritual discernment to recognize the low waves in our lives. This requires regular self-examination, prayer, and time spent in God's Word. The Holy Spirit, who searches all things, can reveal the subtle issues that need our attention (1 Corinthians 2:10).

Once we recognize the low waves, we must address them intentionally. This might involve setting boundaries at work to manage stress, seeking reconciliation in strained relationships, or making time for rest and spiritual renewal. It also means staying vigilant in spiritual practices, even when life seems calm. Regular prayer, worship, and reading of the Scriptures keep us anchored in God's truth and prevent the low waves from eroding our faith.

The Apostle Paul understood the importance of addressing the low waves in his life. Despite facing numerous high waves, including imprisonment, beatings, and shipwrecks, Paul was also mindful of the low waves—the daily pressures and concerns that came with his ministry. He recognized that without the strength of Christ, even these smaller waves could overwhelm him. In 2 Corinthians 12:9-10, Paul writes, "But he said to me,' My grace is sufficient for you, for my power is made perfect in weakness.' Therefore I will boast all the more gladly about my weaknesses so that Christ's power may rest on me." Paul's reliance on God's grace allowed him to withstand the high and low waves of life.

Turning Low Waves Into Opportunities

Just as the high waves offer opportunities for growth and victory, the low waves also have their purpose. They can remind us of our need for God in the everyday aspect of life, keeping us humble and dependent on Him. The low waves can teach us patience, perseverance, and the value of small, consistent efforts in our spiritual journey.

Consider the story of Ruth in the Bible. Ruth's life was not marked by dramatic high waves but by the steady, persistent low waves of hardship, loss, and uncertainty. Yet, through her faithfulness in the mundane tasks of gleaning in the fields and caring for her mother-in-law, Naomi, Ruth positioned herself for God's blessing. Her story demonstrates that even in the low waves of life, when we remain faithful and committed to God's plan, He can turn our seemingly insignificant actions into significant outcomes (Ruth 2-4).

See Paul and the jailer also in **Acts 16:22-27 A lot of people quickly came together there. They started to attack Paul and Silas. So the critical officers said to their soldiers, 'Tear the clothes off, Paul and Silas. Then hit them with sticks!' The soldiers hit Paul and Silas many times. Then they took hold of them, and they pushed them into the prison. The officers told the prison guard, 'Lock the prison door carefully so that these men cannot get free.' The correctional officer did what he had been told to do. He put Paul and Silas in a room in the middle of the prison. He put their feet between big, pieces of wood so they could not move their legs. At midnight, Paul and Silas were praying. They were also singing songs to praise God. The other people in the prison were listening to them. The ground under the prison suddenly shook firmly. Immediately, all the prison doors opened. The chains that held the people in the prison all fell off. The prison guard woke up. He saw that the prison doors were open. He thought that all the people in the prison had become free. He decided that he should kill himself. So he pulled out his sword.** *Easy English Bible*

Paul and Silas were imprisoned, clearly due to Paul disrupting a lucrative business! A young slave girl who earned significant profits for her masters through fortune telling trailed Paul and his companions for several days, (Acts 16:17). After days of enduring this, Paul decided he couldn't take it any longer! Using the authority of Jesus' Name, he expelled the spirit from her, and it departed. This act enraged the owners of the slave girl since they had lost their most significant source of income. Consequently, Paul and Silas were taken before the local authorities and imprisoned. Around midnight, Paul and Silas were praying and singing praises to God. That's the essence of transforming obstacles into opportunities! Isn't it incredible that these faithful individuals faced darkness, evil, and difficult situations, yet they remained unwavering in their praise for the Lord Jesus Christ?

Do you feel the despair in the jailer's heart? He had one primary purpose for living: to be the best Roman jailer possible. He hasn't succeeded in the primary goal of his life. With his motivation for living no longer present, what reason does he have to remain? Some of you might relate to this feeling. You've experienced the loss of something that meant a lot to you, whether it's a relationship, a job, or someone close to you, leaving you to question, "What's the point of going on with life?"
Life encompasses much more than your career, family, and material belongings. If you focus solely on worldly things, you will be unhappy in both this life and the next.

What caused the jailer to shift from feelings of despair to those of assistance and joy instantly? He became aware of his powerless situation! "Gentlemen, what must I do to be saved?" Many of us often need to reach our lowest point before we truly seek a relationship with God! Also, he welcomed Jesus Christ into his life! When the jailer accepted Christ as his Lord and Savior, he experienced a joy in his life that he had never known before. He discovered that Christian joy is influenced not by external situations, but by the internal presence of the Holy Spirit. Suffering arises from depending on ourselves, while happiness is found in trusting the presence and strength of the Holy Spirit. By our own efforts, we cannot find joy, but through faith in Christ, we can experience **"You have never seen Jesus, but still you love him. You do not see him now, but you believe in him. As a result, you are pleased. There are no words to describe how happy you are."** 1 Peter 1:8 *Easy English Bible*

Embracing Both The High And Low Waves

The journey of faith involves navigating both the high and low waves of life with the ultimate aim of triumph. While the high waves test our courage and faith in dramatic ways, the low waves challenge our perseverance, patience, and daily reliance on God. Both are necessary for our growth and maturity as believers.

The key to riding both the high and low waves is to stay anchored in God's Word, remain vigilant in prayer, and continually align ourselves with God's purpose. By doing so, we can withstand the subtle erosions of the low waves and turn them into opportunities for growth, just as we do with the high waves.

As we move forward in our walk with Christ, let us not only brace ourselves for the high waves but also remain mindful of the low waves. In both, God is present, working out His perfect plan for our lives. When we trust Him with the small details as well as the big challenges, we will find that every wave, whether high or low, can carry us closer to our destiny and deeper into His love and grace.

As the curtain closes on life's drama, may you stand triumphant, aligned with God's victorious script.
Amen!

APOSTLE DR. DAVID PHILEMON

CHAPTER ELEVEN

THE FINAL ACT

As the curtains draw near to close on the performance that is your life, it's essential to recognize that every moment, every wave—whether high or low—has been a critical part of God's grand drama. Life's challenges, victories, and even the quiet moments of persistence have been woven into a script that God, the Master Playwright, has crafted with infinite wisdom and love. As an actor in this divine drama, your ultimate success lies in how well you align yourself with God's script, respond to the waves, and fulfill the role you've been given.

The Drama Of Life: Your Role In The Divine Script

Life is not a random series of events but a carefully orchestrated drama, where every actor has a unique role to play. Just as a skilled director guides actors to bring out their best performances, God guides us through the Holy Spirit, encouraging us to trust in His direction, even when the path seems unclear.

Your role in this drama is not a passive one. It requires active participation, faith, and determination. God's script includes moments of triumph and trial, scenes of joy and sorrow, but every line, every act, is designed to bring you closer to your ultimate destiny—eternal fellowship with Him.

The High Waves: Challenges And Triumphs

The high waves of life are those dramatic moments that test the very core of your faith. They are the moments when everything seems to be at stake, and the outcome appears uncertain. These are the times when you must step out in faith, like Peter walking on water, keeping your eyes fixed on Jesus despite the wind and the waves (Matthew 14:28-31).

High waves are often seen as obstacles, but they are also opportunities for God to demonstrate His power and for you to grow in faith. These waves push you beyond your comfort zone, forcing you to rely on God's strength rather than your own. In the final act of your life, how you handle these high waves will determine the impact of your story.

Consider the life of the Apostle Paul. He faced numerous high waves, from shipwrecks and imprisonment to beatings and persecution (2 Corinthians 11:23-28). Yet, through it all, Paul remained steadfast in his faith, trusting in God's script for his life. His perseverance amidst the high waves not only strengthened his faith but also became a powerful testimony that continues to inspire believers today. Paul's life is a vivid illustration of how the high waves, though daunting, are instrumental in shaping a life that honors God.

The Low Waves: The Quiet Strengtheners

While high waves demand immediate attention, low waves—those subtle, ongoing challenges—are equally important in the drama of life. These low waves represent the persistent, everyday trials that test your patience, endurance, and faithfulness. They might not be as dramatic as the high waves, but they play a crucial role in shaping your character and deepening your reliance on God.

In the final act of life, it's easy to overlook the low waves, but they often carry the weight of your testimony. The small decisions you make each day, the quiet acts of obedience, and the consistent practice of faith in the mundane moments all contribute to the strength and stability of your spiritual foundation.

Take, for example, the life of Ruth. Her story is not marked by high waves of dramatic miracles or battles but by steady, low waves of loyalty, hard work, and quiet faithfulness. Ruth's decision to stay with her mother-in-law Naomi, her willingness to glean in the fields, and her humility in following Naomi's guidance all seemed like small, low-wave actions. Yet, these actions positioned Ruth for a significant role in God's plan, as she became the great-grandmother of King David and part of the lineage of Jesus Christ (Ruth 4:13-17).

Aligning With God's Script

As you navigate the waves of life, both high and low, the key to success lies in aligning yourself with God's script. This means surrendering your plans and desires, trusting in God's wisdom, and being obedient to His guidance. Alignment with God's script doesn't mean a life free of challenges; rather, it means that no matter what waves come your way, you can trust that God is using them for your ultimate good and His glory (Romans 8:28).

Aligning with God's script also involves discerning His will through prayer, the study of Scripture, and the counsel of wise, godly people. It means being sensitive to the leading of the Holy Spirit and being willing to adjust your course when God redirects your path. When you align with God's script, you are not just reacting to the waves—you are actively participating in God's plan, playing your role in the divine drama with purpose and conviction.

The Power Of Faith And Determination

In the final act of life, faith and determination are your most powerful tools. Faith allows you to trust in God's script, even when you cannot see the full picture. It is the assurance that, regardless of the waves, God's plan is perfect, and His timing is impeccable. Determination, on the other hand, is the resolve to keep moving forward, to keep playing your part, even when the waves are overwhelming.

Consider the example of Moses, who led the Israelites out of Egypt. His journey was filled with high waves—plagues, the parting of the Red Sea, and the wandering in the wilderness—but it was also marked by low waves, such as the constant complaints of the Israelites and the daily challenges of leadership. Through it all, Moses remained determined to fulfill his role in God's script, trusting that God would lead His people to the Promised Land (Exodus 3:1-12, 14:21-31).

Like Moses, you are called to face the waves with faith and determination, knowing that God is with you every step of the way. Your journey may not be easy, but it is purposeful. Every wave you face is an opportunity to deepen your relationship with God, strengthen your faith, and fulfill the role He has written for you.

The Triumphant Ending

As the final act of your life unfolds, remember that the ending has already been written—and it is triumphant. The ultimate victory was secured through the life, death, and resurrection of Jesus Christ. In Him, you are more than a conqueror, and no wave, no matter how high or low, can separate you from His love (Romans8:37-39).

Your role is to stay aligned with God's script, to trust in His plan, and to act with faith and determination. When you do this, you can face the waves with confidence, knowing that they are not there to destroy you but to propel you toward your destiny.

Stepping Into The Final Act

As you prepare to step into the final act of your life, let the words of Hebrews 12:1-2 be your guide: "Therefore, since we are surrounded by such a great cloud of witnesses, let us throw off everything that hinders and the sin that so easily entangles. And let us run with perseverance the race marked out for us, fixing our eyes on Jesus, the pioneer, and perfecter of faith."

The drama of life, with all its unexpected twists and turns, is not something to be feared. It is a stage upon which God's power and glory are displayed. When we find ourselves facing high waves, let us remember that these are opportunities for God to demonstrate His faithfulness. By trusting in Him and keeping our eyes on Jesus, we can navigate the storms of life with confidence, knowing that our God is greater than any wave that may come our way.

The race has been set before you, the waves are part of the journey, and the final act is approaching. Stand firm in your faith, align with God's script, and let the high and low waves carry you to your ultimate destiny. The stage is set, the script is written, and the victory is assured. Your role is to trust in God, act with determination, and finish strong, knowing that the best is yet to come.

May your life soar above the high waves, discern and conquer the low waves, and rise to the highest heights of your divine destiny fulfillment, firmly anchored in God's script. Amen!

RIDING
THE HIGH
WAVES

May your life soar above
the high waves, discern and
conquer the low waves, and
rise to the highest heights
of your divine destiny
fulfillment, firmly anchored
in God's script.
Amen!

APOSTLE DR. DAVID PHILEMON

CONCLUSION

The gift of stability is one of the most precious gifts God has given us. It allows us to stand firm in the face of life's challenges, remain anchored in His Word, and produce fruit that glorifies Him. In a world that is constantly shifting and changing, stability sets us apart as believers who are not easily shaken. As we build our lives on the solid rock of God's Word, engage in prayer and worship, and foster stability within our communities, we will become immovable, steadfast, and effective in advancing God's kingdom. Stability is not just a gift for our benefit; it is a tool God uses to accomplish His purposes in and through us. Let us embrace this gift, nurture it, and allow it to shape us into the unshakable followers of Christ that God has called us to be.

A SPECIAL INVITATION FROM APOSTLE DR. DAVID PHILEMON

Dear Beloved,

Life's waves can be overwhelming, but the greatest assurance we can have is knowing that we are anchored in Christ. Today, I want to extend to you the most important invitation you will ever receive—the invitation to accept Jesus Christ as your Lord and Savior. No matter where you are or what you've done, God's love for you is unchanging and unfailing. He is calling you to step into a life of purpose, peace, and eternal salvation.

Why Salvation?

Salvation isn't just about heaven; it's about living the full, triumphant life God has planned for you now. It's stepping into His divine script, filled with hope, joy, and fulfillment.

Don't wait for another moment. The waves may be high, but Jesus is reaching out to you right now, ready to pull you up and set your feet on solid ground.

The Salvation Prayer

If you feel a stirring in your heart and are ready to make this life-changing decision, I invite you to pray this prayer with me. Speak these words aloud, and believe them in your heart:

"Heavenly Father, I come to You in the Name of Jesus. I acknowledge that I am a sinner in need of a Savior. I believe that Jesus Christ is Your Son, that He died for my sins, and that You raised Him from the dead. I repent of my sins and turn to You with my whole heart. Jesus, I ask You to come into my life. Be my Lord and my Savior. I surrender my life to You. Fill me with Your Holy Spirit, guide me on the path of righteousness, and help me to follow Your script for my life. Thank You, Father, for saving me. In the name of Jesus. Amen."

Welcome to the Family of God!

If you have just prayed this prayer, **CONGRATULATIONS**! You are now a child of God, and heaven is rejoicing.

Your journey has begun, and we're here to support you as you grow in faith and discover God's amazing plans for your life.

Next Steps:

- Connect with a Bible-Believing Church:

Surround yourself with a community of believers who can support and encourage you in your new walk with Christ.

- Read the Bible Daily: God's Word is your guide. Start with the Gospels (Matthew, Mark, Luke, and John) to learn more about Jesus and His teachings.

- Pray Regularly: Prayer is your lifeline to God. Speak to Him daily, and listen for His voice guiding you.

- Share Your Faith: Don't keep the good news to yourself. Tell others about the amazing decision you've made today.

Tear here

We Want to Hear from You!

If you have prayed this prayer and given your life to Christ, please let us know. We would love to connect with you, provide you with resources, and support you in your spiritual journey. Reach out to us by filling out the form below:

www.ingramcontent.com/pod-product-compliance
Lightning Source LLC
Chambersburg PA
CBHW071901020426
42331CB00010B/2615